Apache HTTP Server 2.2
Official Documentation

Security and Server Programs

Volume II

Fultus™ Books

Apache HTTP Server 2.2

Official Documentation

Security and Server Programs

Volume II

ISBN-10: 1-59682-192-2
ISBN-13: 978-1-59682-192-7

Copyright © 2010 The Apache Software Foundation

Cover design and book layout by Fultus Corporation

Published by Fultus Corporation

Publisher Web: *www.fultus.com*
Linbrary - Linux Library: *www.linbrary.com*
Online Bookstore: *store.fultus.com*
email: *production@fultus.com*

Apache HTTP Server 2.2
Official Documentation List

Version	Title	Edition	ISBN-10	ISBN-13
Apache Web Server 2.2	Apache HTTP Server 2.2 **Vol.I. Server Administration**	paperback	1-59682-191-4	978-1-59682-191-0
		eBook (pdf)	1-59682-195-7	978-1-59682-195-8
	Apache HTTP Server 2.2 **Vol.II. Security & Server Programs**	paperback	1-59682-192-2	978-1-59682-192-7
		eBook (pdf)	1-59682-196-5	978-1-59682-196-5
	Apache HTTP Server 2.2 **Vol.III. Modules (A-H)**	paperback	1-59682-193-0	978-1-59682-193-4
		eBook (pdf)	1-59682-197-3	978-1-59682-197-2
	Apache HTTP Server 2.2 **Vol.IV. Modules (I-V)**	paperback	1-59682-194-9	978-1-59682-194-1
		eBook (pdf)	1-59682-198-1	978-1-59682-198-9
http://www.linbrary.com/apache-http/				

Table of Contents

List of Tables

List of Figures

Part V.
Apache SSL/TLS Encryption

The Apache HTTP Server module `mod_ssl` provides an interface to the *OpenSSL*[1] library, which provides Strong Encryption using the Secure Sockets Layer and Transport Layer Security protocols. The module and this documentation are based on Ralf S. Engelschall's mod_ssl project.

Documentation

- *Introduction*
- *Compatibility*
- *How-To*
- *Frequently Asked Questions*
- *Glossary*

mod_ssl

Extensive documentation on the directives and environment variables provided by this module is provided in the *mod_ssl reference documentation*.

---

[1] *http://www.openssl.org/*

Chapter 39.
SSL/TLS Strong Encryption: An Introduction

The nice thing about standards is that there are so many to choose from. And if you really don't like all the standards you just have to wait another year until the one arises you are looking for.

-- A. Tanenbaum, "Introduction to Computer Networks"

As an introduction this chapter is aimed at readers who are familiar with the Web, HTTP, and Apache, but are not security experts. It is not intended to be a definitive guide to the SSL protocol, nor does it discuss specific techniques for managing certificates in an organization, or the important legal issues of patents and import and export restrictions. Rather, it is intended to provide a common background to mod_ssl users by pulling together various concepts, definitions, and examples as a starting point for further exploration.

The presented content is mainly derived, with the author's permission, from the article *Introducing SSL and Certificates using SSLeay*[1] by *Frederick J. Hirsch*[2], of The Open Group Research Institute, which was published in *Web Security: A Matter of Trust*[3], World Wide Web Journal, Volume 2, Issue 3, Summer 1997. Please send any positive feedback to *Frederick Hirsch*[4] (the original article author) and all negative feedback to *Ralf S. Engelschall*[5] (the mod_ssl author).

39.1. Cryptographic Techniques

Understanding SSL requires an understanding of cryptographic algorithms, message digest functions (aka. one-way or hash functions), and digital signatures. These techniques are the subject of entire books (see for instance [AC96]) and provide the basis for privacy, integrity, and authentication.

---

[1] *http://home.comcast.net/~fjhirsch/Papers/wwwj/*

[2] *http://home.comcast.net/~fjhirsch/*

[3] *http://www.ora.com/catalog/wjsum97/*

[4] *hirsch@fjhirsch.com*

[5] *rse@engelschall.com*

39.1.1. Cryptographic Algorithms

Suppose Alice wants to send a message to her bank to transfer some money. Alice would like the message to be private, since it will include information such as her account number and transfer amount. One solution is to use a cryptographic algorithm, a technique that would transform her message into an encrypted form, unreadable until it is decrypted. Once in this form, the message can only be decrypted by using a secret key. Without the key the message is useless: good cryptographic algorithms make it so difficult for intruders to decode the original text that it isn't worth their effort.

There are two categories of cryptographic algorithms: conventional and public key.

Conventional cryptography

> also known as symmetric cryptography, requires the sender and receiver to share a key: a secret piece of information that may be used to encrypt or decrypt a message. As long as this key is kept secret, nobody other than the sender or recipient can read the message. If Alice and the bank know a secret key, then they can send each other private messages. The task of sharing a key between sender and recipient before communicating, while also keeping it secret from others, can be problematic.

Public key cryptography

> also known as asymmetric cryptography, solves the key exchange problem by defining an algorithm which uses two keys, each of which may be used to encrypt a message. If one key is used to encrypt a message then the other must be used to decrypt it. This makes it possible to receive secure messages by simply publishing one key (the public key) and keeping the other secret (the private key).

Anyone can encrypt a message using the public key, but only the owner of the private key will be able to read it. In this way, Alice can send private messages to the owner of a key-pair (the bank), by encrypting them using their public key. Only the bank will be able to decrypt them.

39.1.2. Message Digests

Although Alice may encrypt her message to make it private, there is still a concern that someone might modify her original message or substitute it with a different one, in order to transfer the money to themselves, for instance. One way of guaranteeing the integrity of Alice's message is for her to create a concise summary of her message and send this to the bank as well. Upon receipt of the message, the bank creates its own summary and compares it with the one Alice sent. If the summaries are the same then the message has been received intact.

A summary such as this is called a *message digest, one-way function* or *hash function*. Message digests are used to create a short, fixed-length representation of a longer, variable-length message. Digest algorithms are designed to produce a unique digest for each message. Message digests are designed to make it impractically difficult to determine the message from the digest and (in theory) impossible to find two different messages which create the same digest -- thus eliminating the possibility of substituting one message for another while maintaining the same digest.

Another challenge that Alice faces is finding a way to send the digest to the bank securely; if the digest is not sent securely, its integrity may be compromised and with it the possibility for the bank to determine the integrity of the original message. Only if the digest is sent securely can the integrity of the associated message be determined.

One way to send the digest securely is to include it in a digital signature.

39.1.3. Digital Signatures

When Alice sends a message to the bank, the bank needs to ensure that the message is really from her, so an intruder cannot request a transaction involving her account. A *digital signature*, created by Alice and included with the message, serves this purpose.

Digital signatures are created by encrypting a digest of the message and other information (such as a sequence number) with the sender's private key. Though anyone can *decrypt* the signature using the public key, only the sender knows the private key. This means that only the sender can have signed the message. Including the digest in the signature means the signature is only good for that message; it also ensures the integrity of the message since no one can change the digest and still sign it.

To guard against interception and reuse of the signature by an intruder at a later date, the signature contains a unique sequence number. This protects the bank from a fraudulent claim from Alice that she did not send the message -- only she could have signed it (non-repudiation).

39.2. Certificates

Although Alice could have sent a private message to the bank, signed it and ensured the integrity of the message, she still needs to be sure that she is really communicating with the bank. This means that she needs to be sure that the public key she is using is part of the bank's key-pair, and not an intruder's. Similarly, the bank needs to verify that the message signature really was signed by the private key that belongs to Alice.

If each party has a certificate which validates the other's identity, confirms the public key and is signed by a trusted agency, then both can be assured that they are communicating with whom they think they are. Such a trusted agency is called a *Certificate Authority* and certificates are used for authentication.

39.2.1. Certificate Contents

A certificate associates a public key with the real identity of an individual, server, or other entity, known as the subject. As shown in *Table 39.1*, information about the subject includes identifying information (the distinguished name) and the public key. It also includes the identification and signature of the Certificate Authority that issued the certificate and the period of time during which the certificate is valid. It may have additional information (or extensions) as well as administrative information for the Certificate Authority's use, such as a serial number.

Subject	Distinguished Name, Public Key
Issuer	Distinguished Name, Signature
Period of Validity	Not Before Date, Not After Date
Administrative Information	Version, Serial Number
Extended Information	Basic Constraints, Netscape Flags, etc.

Table 39.1. Certificate Information

A distinguished name is used to provide an identity in a specific context -- for instance, an individual might have a personal certificate as well as one for their identity as an employee. Distinguished names are defined by the X.509 standard [*X509*], which defines the fields, field names and abbreviations used to refer to the fields (see *Table 39.2*).

DN Field	Abbrev.	Description	Example
Common Name	CN	Name being certified	CN=Joe Average
Organization or Company	O	Name is associated with this organization	O=Snake Oil, Ltd.
Organizational Unit	OU	Name is associated with this organization unit, such as a department	OU=Research Institute
City/Locality	L	Name is located in this City	L=Snake City
State/Province	ST	Name is located in this State/Province	ST=Desert
Country	C	Name is located in this Country (ISO code)	C=XZ

Table 39.2. Distinguished Name Information

A Certificate Authority may define a policy specifying which distinguished field names are optional and which are required. It may also place requirements upon the field contents, as may users of certificates. For example, a Netscape browser requires that the Common Name for a certificate representing a server matches a wildcard pattern for the domain name of that server, such as *.snakeoil.com.

The binary format of a certificate is defined using the ASN.1 notation [*X208*] [*PKCS*]. This notation defines how to specify the contents and encoding rules define how this information is translated into binary form. The binary encoding of the certificate is defined using Distinguished Encoding Rules (DER), which are based on the more general Basic Encoding Rules (BER). For those transmissions which cannot handle binary, the binary form may be translated into an ASCII form by using Base64 encoding [*MIME*]. When placed between begin and end delimiter lines (as below), this encoded version is called a PEM ("Privacy Enhanced Mail") encoded certificate.

Example of a PEM-encoded certificate (snakeoil.crt)

```
-----BEGIN CERTIFICATE-----
MIIC7jCCAlegAwIBAgIBATANBgkqhkiG9w0BAQQFADCBqTELMAkGA1UEBhMCWFkx
FTATBgNVBAgTDFNuYWtlIERlc2VydDETMBEGA1UEBxMKU25ha2UgVG93bjEXMBUG
A1UEChMOU25ha2UgT21sLCBMdGQxHjAcBgNVBAsTFUNlcnRpZmljYXRlIEF1dGhv
cml0eTEVMBMGA1UEAxMMU25ha2UgT21sIENBMR4wHAYJKoZIhvcNAQkBFg9jYUBz
bmFrZW9pbC5kb20wHhcNOTgxMDIxMDg1ODM2WhcNOTkxMDIxMDg1ODM2WjCBpzEL
MAkGA1UEBhMCWFkxFTATBgNVBAgTDFNuYWtlIERlc2VydDETMBEGA1UEBxMKU25h
a2UgVG93bjEXMBUGA1UEChMOU25ha2UgT21sLCBMdGQxFzAVBgNVBAsTD1dlYnNl
cnZlciBUZWFtMRkwFwYDVQQDExB3d3cuc25ha2VvaWwuZG9tMR8wHQYJKoZIhvcN
AQkBFhB3d3dAc25ha2VvaWwuZG9tMIGfMA0GCSqGSIb3DQEBAQUAA4GNADCBiQKB
gQDH9Ge/s2zcH+da+rPTx/DPRp3xGjHZ4GG6pCmvADIEtBtKBFAcZ64n+Dy7Np8b
vKR+yy5DGQiijsH1D/j8HlGE+q4TZ8OFk7BNBFazHxFbYI4OKMiCxdKzdiflyfaa
1WoANFlAzlSdbxeGVHoT0K+gT5w3UxwZKv2DLbCTzLZyPwIDAQABoyYwJDAPBgNV
HRMECDAGAQH/AgEAMBEGCWCGSAGG+EIBAQQEAwIAQDANBgkqhkiG9w0BAQQFAAOB
gQAZUIHAL4D09oE6Lv2k56Gp38OBDuILvwLg1v1KL8mQR+KFjghCrtpqaztZqcDt
2q2QoyulCgSzHbEGmi0EsdkPfg6mp0penssIFePYNI+/8u9HT4LuKMJX15hxBam7
dUHzICxBVC1lnHyYGjDuAMhe3961YAn8bCld1/L4NMGBCQ==
-----END CERTIFICATE-----
```

39.2.2. Certificate Authorities

By verifying the information in a certificate request before granting the certificate, the Certificate Authority assures itself of the identity of the private key owner of a key-pair. For instance, if Alice requests a personal certificate, the Certificate Authority must first make sure that Alice really is the person the certificate request claims she is.

39.2.2.1. Certificate Chains

A Certificate Authority may also issue a certificate for another Certificate Authority. When examining a certificate, Alice may need to examine the certificate of the issuer, for each parent Certificate Authority, until reaching one which she has confidence in. She may decide to trust only certificates with a limited chain of issuers, to reduce her risk of a "bad" certificate in the chain.

39.2.2.2. Creating a Root-Level CA

As noted earlier, each certificate requires an issuer to assert the validity of the identity of the certificate subject, up to the top-level Certificate Authority (CA). This presents a problem: who can vouch for the certificate of the top-level authority, which has no issuer? In this unique case, the certificate is "self-signed", so the issuer of the certificate is the same as the subject. Browsers are preconfigured to trust well-known certificate authorities, but it is important to exercise extra care in trusting a self-signed certificate. The wide publication of a public key by the root authority reduces the risk in trusting this key -- it would be obvious if someone else publicized a key claiming to be the authority.

A number of companies, such as *Thawte*[6] and *VeriSign*[7] have established themselves as Certificate Authorities. These companies provide the following services:

- Verifying certificate requests
- Processing certificate requests
- Issuing and managing certificates

It is also possible to create your own Certificate Authority. Although risky in the Internet environment, it may be useful within an Intranet where the organization can easily verify the identities of individuals and servers.

39.2.2.3. Certificate Management

Establishing a Certificate Authority is a responsibility which requires a solid administrative, technical and management framework. Certificate Authorities not only issue certificates, they also manage them -- that is, they determine for how long certificates remain valid, they renew them and keep lists of certificates that were issued in the past but are no longer valid (Certificate Revocation Lists, or CRLs).

For example, if Alice is entitled to a certificate as an employee of a company but has now left that company, her certificate may need to be revoked. Because certificates are only issued after the subject's identity has been verified and can then be passed around to all those with whom the subject may communicate, it is impossible to tell from the certificate alone that it has been revoked. Therefore when examining certificates for validity it is necessary to contact the issuing Certificate Authority to check CRLs -- this is usually not an automated part of the process.

 Note

> If you use a Certificate Authority that browsers are not configured to trust by default, it is necessary to load the Certificate Authority certificate into the browser,

---

[6] *http://www.thawte.com/*
[7] *http://www.verisign.com/*

enabling the browser to validate server certificates signed by that Certificate Authority. Doing so may be dangerous, since once loaded, the browser will accept all certificates signed by that Certificate Authority.

39.3. Secure Sockets Layer (SSL)

The Secure Sockets Layer protocol is a protocol layer which may be placed between a reliable connection-oriented network layer protocol (e.g. TCP/IP) and the application protocol layer (e.g. HTTP). SSL provides for secure communication between client and server by allowing mutual authentication, the use of digital signatures for integrity and encryption for privacy.

The protocol is designed to support a range of choices for specific algorithms used for cryptography, digests and signatures. This allows algorithm selection for specific servers to be made based on legal, export or other concerns and also enables the protocol to take advantage of new algorithms. Choices are negotiated between client and server when establishing a protocol session.

Version	Source	Description	Browser Support
SSL v2.0	Vendor Standard (from Netscape Corp.) [SSL2]	First SSL protocol for which implementations exist	- NS Navigator 1.x/2.x - MS IE 3.x - Lynx/2.8+OpenSSL
SSL v3.0	Expired Internet Draft (from Netscape Corp.) [SSL3]	Revisions to prevent specific security attacks, add non-RSA ciphers and support for certificate chains	- NS Navigator 2.x/3.x/4.x - MS IE 3.x/4.x - Lynx/2.8+OpenSSL
TLS v1.0	Proposed Internet Standard (from IETF) [TLS1]	Revision of SSL 3.0 to update the MAC layer to HMAC, add block padding for block ciphers, message order standardization and more alert messages.	- Lynx/2.8+OpenSSL

Table 39.3. Versions of the SSL protocol

There are a number of versions of the SSL protocol, as shown in *Table 39.3*. As noted there, one of the benefits in SSL 3.0 is that it adds support of certificate chain loading. This feature allows a server to pass a server certificate along with issuer certificates to the browser. Chain loading also permits the browser to validate the server certificate, even if Certificate Authority certificates are not installed for the intermediate issuers, since they are included in the certificate chain. SSL 3.0 is the basis for the Transport Layer Security [TLS] protocol standard, currently in development by the Internet Engineering Task Force (IETF).

39.3.1. Establishing a Session

The SSL session is established by following a handshake sequence between client and server, as shown in *Figure 39.1*. This sequence may vary, depending on whether the server is configured to provide a server certificate or request a client certificate. Although cases exist where additional handshake steps are required for management of cipher information, this article summarizes one common scenario. See the SSL specification for the full range of possibilities.

 Note

Once an SSL session has been established, it may be reused. This avoids the performance penalty of repeating the many steps needed to start a session. To do this, the server assigns each SSL session a unique session identifier which is cached in the server and which the client can use in future connections to reduce the handshake time (until the session identifer expires from the cache of the server).

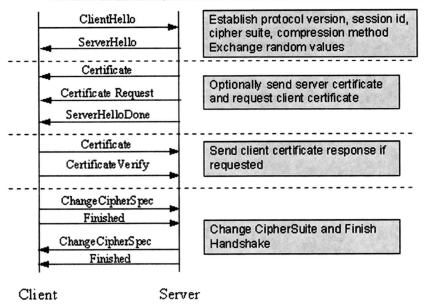

Figure 39.1. Simplified SSL Handshake Sequence

The elements of the handshake sequence, as used by the client and server, are listed below:

1. Negotiate the Cipher Suite to be used during data transfer
2. Establish and share a session key between client and server
3. Optionally authenticate the server to the client
4. Optionally authenticate the client to the server

The first step, Cipher Suite Negotiation, allows the client and server to choose a Cipher Suite supported by both of them. The SSL3.0 protocol specification defines 31 Cipher Suites. A Cipher Suite is defined by the following components:

- Key Exchange Method
- Cipher for Data Transfer
- Message Digest for creating the Message Authentication Code (MAC)

These three elements are described in the sections that follow.

39.3.2. Key Exchange Method

The key exchange method defines how the shared secret symmetric cryptography key used for application data transfer will be agreed upon by client and server. SSL 2.0 uses RSA key exchange only, while SSL 3.0 supports a choice of key exchange algorithms including RSA key exchange (when certificates are used), and Diffie-Hellman key exchange (for exchanging keys without certificates, or without prior communication between client and server).

One variable in the choice of key exchange methods is digital signatures -- whether or not to use them, and if so, what kind of signatures to use. Signing with a private key provides protection against a man-in-the-middle-attack during the information exchange used to generating the shared key [AC96, p516].

39.3.3. Cipher for Data Transfer

SSL uses conventional symmetric cryptography, as described earlier, for encrypting messages in a session. There are nine choices of how to encrypt, including the option not to encrypt:

- No encryption
- Stream Ciphers
  - RC4 with 40-bit keys
  - RC4 with 128-bit keys
- CBC Block Ciphers
  - RC2 with 40 bit key
  - DES with 40 bit key
  - DES with 56 bit key
  - Triple-DES with 168 bit key
  - Idea (128 bit key)
  - Fortezza (96 bit key)

"CBC" refers to Cipher Block Chaining, which means that a portion of the previously encrypted cipher text is used in the encryption of the current block. "DES" refers to the Data

Encryption Standard [*AC96*, ch12], which has a number of variants (including DES40 and 3DES_EDE). "Idea" is currently one of the best and cryptographically strongest algorithms available, and "RC2" is a proprietary algorithm from RSA DSI [*AC96*, ch13].

39.3.4. Digest Function

The choice of digest function determines how a digest is created from a record unit. SSL supports the following:

- No digest (Null choice)
- MD5, a 128-bit hash
- Secure Hash Algorithm (SHA-1), a 160-bit hash

The message digest is used to create a Message Authentication Code (MAC) which is encrypted with the message to verify integrity and to protect against replay attacks.

39.3.5. Handshake Sequence Protocol

The handshake sequence uses three protocols:

- The *SSL Handshake Protocol* for performing the client and server SSL session establishment.
- The *SSL Change Cipher Spec Protocol* for actually establishing agreement on the Cipher Suite for the session.
- The *SSL Alert Protocol* for conveying SSL error messages between client and server.

These protocols, as well as application protocol data, are encapsulated in the *SSL Record Protocol*, as shown in *Figure 39.2*. An encapsulated protocol is transferred as data by the lower layer protocol, which does not examine the data. The encapsulated protocol has no knowledge of the underlying protocol.

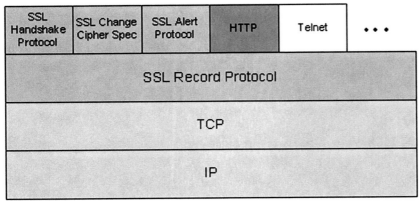

Figure 39.2. SSL Protocol Stack

The encapsulation of SSL control protocols by the record protocol means that if an active session is renegotiated the control protocols will be transmitted securely. If there was no previous session, the Null cipher suite is used, which means there will be no encryption and messages will have no integrity digests, until the session has been established.

39.3.6. Data Transfer

The SSL Record Protocol, shown in *Figure 39.3*, is used to transfer application and SSL Control data between the client and server, where necessary fragmenting this data into smaller units, or combining multiple higher level protocol data messages into single units. It may compress, attach digest signatures, and encrypt these units before transmitting them using the underlying reliable transport protocol (Note: currently, no major SSL implementations include support for compression).

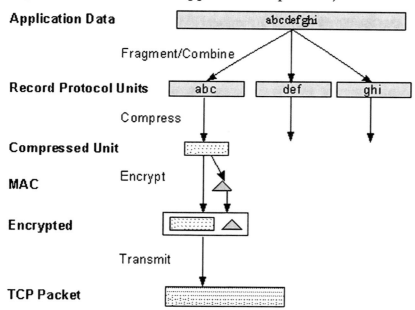

Figure 39.3. SSL Record Protocol

39.3.7. Securing HTTP Communication

One common use of SSL is to secure Web HTTP communication between a browser and a webserver. This does not preclude the use of non-secured HTTP - the secure version (called HTTPS) is the same as plain HTTP over SSL, but uses the URL scheme https rather than http, and a different server port (by default, port 443). This functionality is a large part of what mod_ssl provides for the Apache webserver.

39.4. References

[AC96]

Bruce Schneier, Applied Cryptography, 2nd Edition, Wiley, 1996. See
http://www.counterpane.com/ for various other materials by Bruce Schneier.

[X208]

ITU-T Recommendation X.208, Specification of Abstract Syntax Notation One (ASN.1),
1988. See for instance *http://www.itu.int/rec/recommendation.asp?type=items&lang=
e&parent=T-REC-X.208-198811-I.*

[X509]

ITU-T Recommendation X.509, The Directory - Authentication Framework. See for
instance *http://www.itu.int/rec/recommendation.asp?type=folders&lang=e&parent=T-REC-
X.509.*

[PKCS]

Public Key Cryptography Standards (PKCS), RSA Laboratories Technical Notes, See
http://www.rsasecurity.com/rsalabs/pkcs/.

[MIME]

N. Freed, N. Borenstein, Multipurpose Internet Mail Extensions (MIME) Part One:
Format of Internet Message Bodies, RFC2045. See for instance *http://ietf.org/rfc/rfc2045.txt.*

[SSL2]

Kipp E.B. Hickman, The SSL Protocol, 1995. See
http://www.netscape.com/eng/security/SSL_2.html.

[SSL3]

Alan O. Freier, Philip Karlton, Paul C. Kocher, The SSL Protocol Version 3.0, 1996. See
http://www.netscape.com/eng/ssl3/draft302.txt.

[TLS1]

Tim Dierks, Christopher Allen, The TLS Protocol Version 1.0, 1999. See
http://ietf.org/rfc/rfc2246.txt.

Chapter 40.
SSL/TLS Strong Encryption: Compatibility

All PCs are compatible. But some of them are more compatible than others.

-- Unknown

This page covers backwards compatibility between mod_ssl and other SSL solutions. mod_ssl is not the only SSL solution for Apache; four additional products are (or were) also available: Ben Laurie's freely available *Apache-SSL*[1] (from where mod_ssl were originally derived in 1998), Red Hat's commercial *Secure Web Server*[2] (which was based on mod_ssl), Covalent's commercial *Raven SSL Module*[3] (also based on mod_ssl) and finally C2Net's (now Red Hat's) commercial product *Stronghold*[4] (based on a different evolution branch named Sioux up to Stronghold 2.x and based on mod_ssl since Stronghold 3.x).

mod_ssl mostly provides a superset of the functionality of all the other solutions, so it's simple to migrate from one of the older modules to mod_ssl. The configuration directives and environment variable names used by the older SSL solutions vary from those used in mod_ssl; mapping tables are included here to give the equivalents used by mod_ssl.

40.1. Configuration Directives

The mapping between configuration directives used by Apache-SSL 1.x and mod_ssl 2.0.x is given in *Table 40.1*. The mapping from Sioux 1.x and Stronghold 2.x is only partial because of special functionality in these interfaces which mod_ssl doesn't provide.

Old Directive	mod_ssl Directive	Comment
Apache-SSL 1.x & mod_ssl 2.0.x compatibility:		
SSLEnable	SSLEngine on	compactified
SSLDisable	SSLEngine off	compactified
SSLLogFile *file*	SSLLog *file*	compactified

---

[1] *http://www.apache-ssl.org/*

[2] *http://www.redhat.com/products/product-details.phtml?id=rhsa*

[3] *http://www.covalent.net/*

[4] *http://www.redhat.com/explore/stronghold/*

Old Directive	mod_ssl Directive	Comment
SSLRequiredCiphers *spec*	SSLCipherSuite *spec*	renamed
SSLRequireCipher *c1* ...	SSLRequire %{SSL_CIPHER} in {"*c1*", ...}	generalized
SSLBanCipher *c1* ...	SSLRequire not (%{SSL_CIPHER} in {"*c1*", ...})	generalized
SSLFakeBasicAuth	SSLOptions +FakeBasicAuth	merged
SSLCacheServerPath *dir*	-	functionality removed
SSLCacheServerPort *integer*	-	functionality removed
Apache-SSL 1.x compatibility:		
SSLExportClientCertificates	SSLOptions +ExportCertData	merged
SSLCacheServerRunDir *dir*	-	functionality not supported
Sioux 1.x compatibility:		
SSL_CertFile *file*	SSLCertificateFile *file*	renamed
SSL_KeyFile *file*	SSLCertificateKeyFile *file*	renamed
SSL_CipherSuite *arg*	SSLCipherSuite *arg*	renamed
SSL_X509VerifyDir *arg*	SSLCACertificatePath *arg*	renamed
SSL_Log *file*	SSLLogFile *file*	renamed
SSL_Connect *flag*	SSLEngine *flag*	renamed
SSL_ClientAuth *arg*	SSLVerifyClient *arg*	renamed
SSL_X509VerifyDepth *arg*	SSLVerifyDepth *arg*	renamed
SSL_FetchKeyPhraseFrom *arg*	-	not directly mappable; use SSLPassPhraseDialog
SSL_SessionDir *dir*	-	not directly mappable; use SSLSessionCache
SSL_Require *expr*	-	not directly mappable; use SSLRequire
SSL_CertFileType *arg*	-	functionality not supported
SSL_KeyFileType *arg*	-	functionality not supported
SSL_X509VerifyPolicy *arg*	-	functionality not supported
SSL_LogX509Attributes *arg*	-	functionality not supported
Stronghold 2.x compatibility:		
StrongholdAccelerator *engine*	SSLCryptoDevice *engine*	renamed

Old Directive	mod_ssl Directive	Comment
StrongholdKey *dir*	-	functionality not needed
StrongholdLicenseFile *dir*	-	functionality not needed
SSLFlag *flag*	SSLEngine *flag*	renamed
SSLSessionLockFile *file*	SSLMutex *file*	renamed
SSLCipherList *spec*	SSLCipherSuite *spec*	renamed
RequireSSL	SSLRequireSSL	renamed
SSLErrorFile *file*	-	functionality not supported
SSLRoot *dir*	-	functionality not supported
SSL_CertificateLogDir *dir*	-	functionality not supported
AuthCertDir *dir*	-	functionality not supported
SSL_Group *name*	-	functionality not supported
SSLProxyMachineCertPath *dir*	SSLProxyMachineCertificatePath *dir*	renamed
SSLProxyMachineCertFile *file*	SSLProxyMachineCertificateFile *file*	renamed
SSLProxyCipherList *spec*	SSLProxyCipherSpec *spec*	renamed

Table 40.1. Configuration Directive Mapping

40.2. Environment Variables

The mapping between environment variable names used by the older SSL solutions and the names used by mod_ssl is given in *Table 40.2*.

Old Variable	mod_ssl Variable	Comment
SSL_PROTOCOL_VERSION	SSL_PROTOCOL	renamed
SSLEAY_VERSION	SSL_VERSION_LIBRARY	renamed
HTTPS_SECRETKEYSIZE	SSL_CIPHER_USEKEYSIZE	renamed
HTTPS_KEYSIZE	SSL_CIPHER_ALGKEYSIZE	renamed
HTTPS_CIPHER	SSL_CIPHER	renamed
HTTPS_EXPORT	SSL_CIPHER_EXPORT	renamed
SSL_SERVER_KEY_SIZE	SSL_CIPHER_ALGKEYSIZE	renamed
SSL_SERVER_CERTIFICATE	SSL_SERVER_CERT	renamed
SSL_SERVER_CERT_START	SSL_SERVER_V_START	renamed
SSL_SERVER_CERT_END	SSL_SERVER_V_END	renamed
SSL_SERVER_CERT_SERIAL	SSL_SERVER_M_SERIAL	renamed

Old Variable	mod_ssl Variable	Comment
SSL_SERVER_SIGNATURE_ALGORITHM	SSL_SERVER_A_SIG	renamed
SSL_SERVER_DN	SSL_SERVER_S_DN	renamed
SSL_SERVER_CN	SSL_SERVER_S_DN_CN	renamed
SSL_SERVER_EMAIL	SSL_SERVER_S_DN_Email	renamed
SSL_SERVER_O	SSL_SERVER_S_DN_O	renamed
SSL_SERVER_OU	SSL_SERVER_S_DN_OU	renamed
SSL_SERVER_C	SSL_SERVER_S_DN_C	renamed
SSL_SERVER_SP	SSL_SERVER_S_DN_SP	renamed
SSL_SERVER_L	SSL_SERVER_S_DN_L	renamed
SSL_SERVER_IDN	SSL_SERVER_I_DN	renamed
SSL_SERVER_ICN	SSL_SERVER_I_DN_CN	renamed
SSL_SERVER_IEMAIL	SSL_SERVER_I_DN_Email	renamed
SSL_SERVER_IO	SSL_SERVER_I_DN_O	renamed
SSL_SERVER_IOU	SSL_SERVER_I_DN_OU	renamed
SSL_SERVER_IC	SSL_SERVER_I_DN_C	renamed
SSL_SERVER_ISP	SSL_SERVER_I_DN_SP	renamed
SSL_SERVER_IL	SSL_SERVER_I_DN_L	renamed
SSL_CLIENT_CERTIFICATE	SSL_CLIENT_CERT	renamed
SSL_CLIENT_CERT_START	SSL_CLIENT_V_START	renamed
SSL_CLIENT_CERT_END	SSL_CLIENT_V_END	renamed
SSL_CLIENT_CERT_SERIAL	SSL_CLIENT_M_SERIAL	renamed
SSL_CLIENT_SIGNATURE_ALGORITHM	SSL_CLIENT_A_SIG	renamed
SSL_CLIENT_DN	SSL_CLIENT_S_DN	renamed
SSL_CLIENT_CN	SSL_CLIENT_S_DN_CN	renamed
SSL_CLIENT_EMAIL	SSL_CLIENT_S_DN_Email	renamed
SSL_CLIENT_O	SSL_CLIENT_S_DN_O	renamed
SSL_CLIENT_OU	SSL_CLIENT_S_DN_OU	renamed
SSL_CLIENT_C	SSL_CLIENT_S_DN_C	renamed
SSL_CLIENT_SP	SSL_CLIENT_S_DN_SP	renamed
SSL_CLIENT_L	SSL_CLIENT_S_DN_L	renamed
SSL_CLIENT_IDN	SSL_CLIENT_I_DN	renamed
SSL_CLIENT_ICN	SSL_CLIENT_I_DN_CN	renamed
SSL_CLIENT_IEMAIL	SSL_CLIENT_I_DN_Email	renamed

Old Variable	mod_ssl Variable	Comment
SSL_CLIENT_IO	SSL_CLIENT_I_DN_O	renamed
SSL_CLIENT_IOU	SSL_CLIENT_I_DN_OU	renamed
SSL_CLIENT_IC	SSL_CLIENT_I_DN_C	renamed
SSL_CLIENT_ISP	SSL_CLIENT_I_DN_SP	renamed
SSL_CLIENT_IL	SSL_CLIENT_I_DN_L	renamed
SSL_EXPORT	SSL_CIPHER_EXPORT	renamed
SSL_KEYSIZE	SSL_CIPHER_ALGKEYSIZE	renamed
SSL_SECKEYSIZE	SSL_CIPHER_USEKEYSIZE	renamed
SSL_SSLEAY_VERSION	SSL_VERSION_LIBRARY	renamed
SSL_STRONG_CRYPTO	-	Not supported by mod_ssl
SSL_SERVER_KEY_EXP	-	Not supported by mod_ssl
SSL_SERVER_KEY_ALGORITHM	-	Not supported by mod_ssl
SSL_SERVER_KEY_SIZE	-	Not supported by mod_ssl
SSL_SERVER_SESSIONDIR	-	Not supported by mod_ssl
SSL_SERVER_CERTIFICATELOGDIR	-	Not supported by mod_ssl
SSL_SERVER_CERTFILE	-	Not supported by mod_ssl
SSL_SERVER_KEYFILE	-	Not supported by mod_ssl
SSL_SERVER_KEYFILETYPE	-	Not supported by mod_ssl
SSL_CLIENT_KEY_EXP	-	Not supported by mod_ssl
SSL_CLIENT_KEY_ALGORITHM	-	Not supported by mod_ssl
SSL_CLIENT_KEY_SIZE	-	Not supported by mod_ssl

Table 40.2. Environment Variable Derivation

40.3. Custom Log Functions

When mod_ssl is enabled, additional functions exist for the *Custom Log Format* of
mod_log_config as documented in the Reference Chapter. Beside the "%{*varname*}x"
eXtension format function which can be used to expand any variables provided by any
module, an additional Cryptography "%{*name*}c" cryptography format function exists for
backward compatibility. The currently implemented function calls are listed in *Table 40.3*.

Function Call	Description
%...{version}c	SSL protocol version
%...{cipher}c	SSL cipher

Function Call	Description
%...{subjectdn}c	Client Certificate Subject Distinguished Name
%...{issuerdn}c	Client Certificate Issuer Distinguished Name
%...{errcode}c	Certificate Verification Error (numerical)
%...{errstr}c	Certificate Verification Error (string)

Table 40.3. Custom Log Cryptography Fu

Chapter 41.
SSL/TLS Strong Encryption: How-To

The solution to this problem is trivial and is left as an exercise for the reader.

-- Standard textbook cookie

How to solve particular security problems for an SSL-aware webserver is not always obvious because of the interactions between SSL, HTTP and Apache's way of processing requests. This chapter gives instructions on how to solve some typical situations. Treat it as a first step to find out the final solution, but always try to understand the stuff before you use it. Nothing is worse than using a security solution without knowing its restrictions and how it interacts with other systems.

41.1. Cipher Suites and Enforcing Strong Security

- *How can I create a real SSLv2-only server?*
- *How can I create an SSL server which accepts strong encryption only?*
- *How can I create an SSL server which accepts strong encryption only, but allows export browsers to upgrade to stronger encryption?*
- *How can I create an SSL server which accepts all types of ciphers in general, but requires a strong cipher for access to a particular URL?*

How can I create a real SSLv2-only server?

The following creates an SSL server which speaks only the SSLv2 protocol and its ciphers.

httpd.conf

```
SSLProtocol -all +SSLv2
SSLCipherSuite SSLv2:+HIGH:+MEDIUM:+LOW:+EXP
```

How can I create an SSL server which accepts strong encryption only?

The following enables only the seven strongest ciphers:

httpd.conf

```
SSLProtocol all
SSLCipherSuite HIGH:MEDIUM
```

How can I create an SSL server which accepts strong encryption only, but allows export browsers to upgrade to stronger encryption?

This facility is called Server Gated Cryptography (SGC) and requires a Global ID server certificate, signed by a special CA certificate from Verisign. This enables strong encryption in 'export' versions of browsers, which traditionally could not support it (because of US export restrictions).

When a browser connects with an export cipher, the server sends its Global ID certificate. The browser verifies this, and can then upgrade its cipher suite before any HTTP communication takes place. The problem lies in allowing browsers to upgrade in this fashion, but still requiring strong encryption. In other words, we want browsers to either start a connection with strong encryption, or to start with export ciphers but upgrade to strong encryption before beginning HTTP communication.

This can be done as follows:

```
httpd.conf
# allow all ciphers for the initial handshake,
# so export browsers can upgrade via SGC facility
SSLCipherSuite ALL:!ADH:RC4+RSA:+HIGH:+MEDIUM:+LOW:+SSLv2:+EXP:+eNULL

<Directory /usr/local/apache2/htdocs>
# but finally deny all browsers which haven't upgraded
SSLRequire %{SSL_CIPHER_USEKEYSIZE} >= 128
</Directory>
```

How can I create an SSL server which accepts all types of ciphers in general, but requires a strong ciphers for access to a particular URL?

Obviously, a server-wide SSLCipherSuite which restricts ciphers to the strong variants, isn't the answer here. However, mod_ssl can be reconfigured within Location blocks, to give a per-directory solution, and can automatically force a renegotiation of the SSL parameters to meet the new configuration. This can be done as follows:

```
# be liberal in general
SSLCipherSuite ALL:!ADH:RC4+RSA:+HIGH:+MEDIUM:+LOW:+SSLv2:+EXP:+eNULL

<Location /strong/area>
# but https://hostname/strong/area/ and below
# requires strong ciphers
SSLCipherSuite HIGH:MEDIUM
</Location>
```

41.2. Client Authentication and Access Control

- *How can I force clients to authenticate using certificates?*
- *How can I force clients to authenticate using certificates for a particular URL, but still allow arbitrary clients to access the rest of the server?*
- *How can I allow only clients who have certificates to access a particular URL, but allow all clients to access the rest of the server?*
- *How can I require HTTPS with strong ciphers, and either basic authentication or client certificates, for access to part of the Intranet website, for clients coming from the Internet?*

How can I force clients to authenticate using certificates?

When you know all of your users (eg, as is often the case on a corporate Intranet), you can require plain certificate authentication. All you need to do is to create client certificates signed by your own CA certificate (ca.crt) and then verify the clients against this certificate.

httpd.conf
```
# require a client certificate which has to be directly
# signed by our CA certificate in ca.crt
SSLVerifyClient require
SSLVerifyDepth 1
SSLCACertificateFile conf/ssl.crt/ca.crt
```

How can I force clients to authenticate using certificates for a particular URL, but still allow arbitrary clients to access the rest of the server?

To force clients to authenticate using certificates for a particular URL, you can use the per-directory reconfiguration features of mod_ssl:

httpd.conf
```
SSLVerifyClient none
SSLCACertificateFile conf/ssl.crt/ca.crt

<Location /secure/area>
SSLVerifyClient require
SSLVerifyDepth 1
</Location>
```

How can I allow only clients who have certificates to access a particular URL, but allow all clients to access the rest of the server?

The key to doing this is checking that part of the client certificate matches what you expect. Usually this means checking all or part of the Distinguished Name (DN), to see if it contains some known string. There are two ways to do this, using either mod_auth_basic or SSLRequire.

The mod_auth_basic method is generally required when the certificates are completely arbitrary, or when their DNs have no common fields (usually the organisation, etc.). In this case, you should establish a password database containing *all* clients allowed, as follows:

httpd.conf

```
SSLVerifyClient         none
<Directory /usr/local/apache2/htdocs/secure/area>
SSLVerifyClient         require
SSLVerifyDepth          5
SSLCACertificateFile conf/ssl.crt/ca.crt
SSLCACertificatePath conf/ssl.crt
SSLOptions              +FakeBasicAuth
SSLRequireSSL
AuthName                "Snake Oil Authentication"
AuthType                Basic
AuthBasicProvider       file
AuthUserFile            /usr/local/apache2/conf/httpd.passwd
Require                 valid-user
</Directory>
```

The password used in this example is the DES encrypted string "password". See the SSLOptions docs for more information.

httpd.passwd

```
/C=DE/L=Munich/O=Snake Oil, Ltd./OU=Staff/CN=Foo:xxj31ZMTZzkVA
/C=US/L=S.F./O=Snake Oil, Ltd./OU=CA/CN=Bar:xxj31ZMTZzkVA
/C=US/L=L.A./O=Snake Oil, Ltd./OU=Dev/CN=Quux:xxj31ZMTZzkVA
```

When your clients are all part of a common hierarchy, which is encoded into the DN, you can match them more easily using SSLRequire, as follows:

httpd.conf

```
SSLVerifyClient         none
<Directory /usr/local/apache2/htdocs/secure/area>
  SSLVerifyClient         require
  SSLVerifyDepth          5
  SSLCACertificateFile conf/ssl.crt/ca.crt
```

```
SSLCACertificatePath conf/ssl.crt
SSLOptions          +FakeBasicAuth
SSLRequireSSL
SSLRequire          %{SSL_CLIENT_S_DN_O}  eq "Snake Oil, Ltd." \
          and %{SSL_CLIENT_S_DN_OU} in {"Staff", "CA", "Dev"}
</Directory>
```

How can I require HTTPS with strong ciphers, and either basic authentication or client certificates, for access to part of the Intranet website, for clients coming from the Internet? I still want to allow plain HTTP access for clients on the Intranet.

These examples presume that clients on the Intranet have IPs in the range 192.168.1.0/24, and that the part of the Intranet website you want to allow internet access to is /usr/local/apache2/htdocs/subarea. This configuration should remain outside of your HTTPS virtual host, so that it applies to both HTTPS and HTTP.

httpd.conf

```
SSLCACertificateFile conf/ssl.crt/company-ca.crt

<Directory /usr/local/apache2/htdocs>
#   Outside the subarea only Intranet access is granted
Order               deny,allow
Deny                from all
Allow               from 192.168.1.0/24
</Directory>

<Directory /usr/local/apache2/htdocs/subarea>
#   Inside the subarea any Intranet access is allowed
#   but from the Internet only HTTPS + Strong-Cipher + Password
#   or the alternative HTTPS + Strong-Cipher + Client-Certificate

#   If HTTPS is used, make sure a strong cipher is used.
#   Additionally allow client certs as alternative to basic auth.
SSLVerifyClient     optional
SSLVerifyDepth      1
SSLOptions          +FakeBasicAuth +StrictRequire
SSLRequire          %{SSL_CIPHER_USEKEYSIZE} >= 128

#   Force clients from the Internet to use HTTPS
RewriteEngine       on
RewriteCond         %{REMOTE_ADDR} !^192\.168\.1\.[0-9]+$
RewriteCond         %{HTTPS} !=on
RewriteRule         .* - [F]
```

```
#    Allow Network Access and/or Basic Auth
Satisfy              any

#    Network Access Control
Order                deny,allow
Deny                 from all
Allow                192.168.1.0/24

#    HTTP Basic Authentication
AuthType             basic
AuthName             "Protected Intranet Area"
AuthBasicProvider    file
AuthUserFile         conf/protected.passwd
Require              valid-user
</Directory>
```

Chapter 42.
SSL/TLS Strong Encryption: FAQ

The wise man doesn't give the right answers, he poses the right questions.

-- Claude Levi-Strauss

This chapter is a collection of frequently asked questions (FAQ) and corresponding answers following the popular USENET tradition. Most of these questions occurred on the Newsgroup *comp.infosystems.www.servers.unix* or the mod_ssl Support Mailing List *modssl-users@modssl.org*. They are collected at this place to avoid answering the same questions over and over.

Please read this chapter at least once when installing mod_ssl or at least search for your problem here before submitting a problem report to the author.

42.1. About The Module

- *What is the history of mod_ssl?*
- *mod_ssl and Wassenaar Arrangement?*

What is the history of mod_ssl?

The mod_ssl v1 package was initially created in April 1998 by *Ralf S. Engelschall*[1] via porting *Ben Laurie's*[2] *Apache-SSL*[3] 1.17 source patches for Apache 1.2.6 to Apache 1.3b6. Because of conflicts with Ben Laurie's development cycle it then was re-assembled from scratch for Apache 1.3.0 by merging the old mod_ssl 1.x with the newer Apache-SSL 1.18. From this point on mod_ssl lived its own life as mod_ssl v2. The first publicly released version was mod_ssl 2.0.0 from August 10th, 1998.

After US export restrictions on cryptographic software were loosened, mod_ssl became part of the Apache HTTP Server with the release of Apache httpd 2.

---

[1] *rse@engelschall.com*
[2] *ben@algroup.co.uk*
[3] *http://www.apache-ssl.org/*

Is mod_ssl affected by the Wassenaar Arrangement?

First, let us explain what *Wassenaar* and its *Arrangement on Export Controls for Conventional Arms and Dual-Use Goods and Technologies* is: This is a international regime, established in 1995, to control trade in conventional arms and dual-use goods and technology. It replaced the previous *CoCom* regime. Further details on both the Arrangement and its signatories are available at *http://www.wassenaar.org/*.

In short, the aim of the Wassenaar Arrangement is to prevent the build up of military capabilities that threaten regional and international security and stability. The Wassenaar Arrangement controls the export of cryptography as a dual-use good, that is, something that has both military and civilian applications. However, the Wassenaar Arrangement also provides an exemption from export controls for mass-market software and free software.

In the current Wassenaar *List of Dual Use Goods and Technologies And Munitions*, under GENERAL SOFTWARE NOTE (GSN) it says The Lists do not control "software" which is either: 1. [...] 2. "in the public domain". And under DEFINITIONS OF TERMS USED IN THESE LISTS we find In the public domain defined as "technology" or "software" which has been made available without restrictions upon its further dissemination. Note: Copyright restrictions do not remove "technology" or "software" from being "in the public domain".

So, both mod_ssl and OpenSSL are in the public domain for the purposes of the Wassenaar Arrangement and its List of Dual Use Goods and Technologies And Munitions List, and thus not affected by its provisions.

42.2. Installation

- *Why do I get permission errors related to SSLMutex when I start Apache?*
- *Why does mod_ssl stop with the error "Failed to generate temporary 512 bit RSA private key" when I start Apache?*

Why do I get permission errors related to SSLMutex when I start Apache?

Errors such as "mod_ssl: Child could not open SSLMutex lockfile /opt/apache/logs/ssl_mutex.18332 (System error follows) [...] System: Permission denied (errno: 13)" are usually caused by overly restrictive permissions on the *parent* directories. Make sure that all parent directories (here /opt, /opt/apache and /opt/apache/logs) have the x-bit set for, at minimum, the UID under which Apache's children are running (see the User directive).

Why does mod_ssl stop with the error "Failed to generate temporary 512 bit RSA private key" when I start Apache?

Cryptographic software needs a source of unpredictable data to work correctly. Many open source operating systems provide a "randomness device" that serves this purpose (usually named /dev/random). On other systems, applications have to seed the OpenSSL Pseudo Random Number Generator (PRNG) manually with appropriate data before generating keys or performing public key encryption. As of version 0.9.5, the OpenSSL functions that need randomness report an error if the PRNG has not been seeded with at least 128 bits of randomness.

To prevent this error, mod_ssl has to provide enough entropy to the PRNG to allow it to work correctly. This can be done via the SSLRandomSeed directive.

42.3. Configuration

- *Is it possible to provide HTTP and HTTPS from the same server?*
- *Which port does HTTPS use?*
- *How do I speak HTTPS manually for testing purposes?*
- *Why does the connection hang when I connect to my SSL-aware Apache server?*
- *Why do I get "Connection Refused" errors, when trying to access my newly installed Apache+mod_ssl server via HTTPS?*
- *Why are the SSL_XXX variables not available to my CGI & SSI scripts?*
- *How can I switch between HTTP and HTTPS in relative hyperlinks?*

Is it possible to provide HTTP and HTTPS from the same server?

Yes. HTTP and HTTPS use different server ports (HTTP binds to port 80, HTTPS to port 443), so there is no direct conflict between them. You can either run two separate server instances bound to these ports, or use Apache's elegant virtual hosting facility to create two virtual servers, both served by the same instance of Apache - one responding over HTTP to requests on port 80, and the other responding over HTTPS to requests on port 443.

Which port does HTTPS use?

You can run HTTPS on any port, but the standards specify port 443, which is where any HTTPS compliant browser will look by default. You can force your browser to look on a different port by specifying it in the URL. For example, if your server is set up to serve pages over HTTPS on port 8080, you can access them at https://example.com:8080/

How do I speak HTTPS manually for testing purposes?

While you usually just use

```
$ telnet localhost 80
GET / HTTP/1.0
```

for simple testing of Apache via HTTP, it's not so easy for HTTPS because of the SSL protocol between TCP and HTTP. With the help of OpenSSL's s_client command, however, you can do a similar check via HTTPS:

```
$ openssl s_client -connect localhost:443 -state -debug
GET / HTTP/1.0
```

Before the actual HTTP response you will receive detailed information about the SSL handshake. For a more general command line client which directly understands both HTTP and HTTPS, can perform GET and POST operations, can use a proxy, supports byte ranges, etc. you should have a look at the nifty *cURL*[4] tool. Using this, you can check that Apache is responding correctly to requests via HTTP and HTTPS as follows:

```
$ curl http://localhost/
$ curl https://localhost/
```

Why does the connection hang when I connect to my SSL-aware Apache server?

This can happen when you try to connect to a HTTPS server (or virtual server) via HTTP (eg, using *http://example.com/* instead of *https://example.com*). It can also happen when trying to connect via HTTPS to a HTTP server (eg, using *https://example.com/* on a server which doesn't support HTTPS, or which supports it on a non-standard port). Make sure that you're connecting to a (virtual) server that supports SSL.

Why do I get "Connection Refused" messages, when trying to access my newly installed Apache+mod_ssl server via HTTPS?

This error can be caused by an incorrect configuration. Please make sure that your <u>Listen</u> directives match your <u><VirtualHost></u> directives. If all else fails, please start afresh, using the default configuration provided by <u>mod_ssl</u>.

---

[4] *http://curl.haxx.se/*

Why are the `ssl_xxx` variables not available to my CGI & SSI scripts?

Please make sure you have "`SSLOptions +StdEnvVars`" enabled for the context of your CGI/SSI requests.

How can I switch between HTTP and HTTPS in relative hyperlinks?

Usually, to switch between HTTP and HTTPS, you have to use fully-qualified hyperlinks (because you have to change the URL scheme). Using `mod_rewrite` however, you can manipulate relative hyperlinks, to achieve the same effect.

```
RewriteEngine on
RewriteRule ^/(.*):SSL$ https://%{SERVER_NAME}/$1 [R,L]
RewriteRule ^/(.*):NOSSL$ http://%{SERVER_NAME}/$1 [R,L]
```

This rewrite ruleset lets you use hyperlinks of the form `<a href="document.html:SSL">`, to switch to HTTPS in a relative link. (Replace SSL with NOSSL to switch to HTTP.)

42.4. Certificates

- *What are RSA Private Keys, CSRs and Certificates?*
- *Is there a difference on startup between a non-SSL-aware Apache and an SSL-aware Apache?*
- *How do I create a self-signed SSL Certificate for testing purposes?*
- *How do I create a real SSL Certificate?*
- *How do I create and use my own Certificate Authority (CA)?*
- *How can I change the pass-phrase on my private key file?*
- *How can I get rid of the pass-phrase dialog at Apache startup time?*
- *How do I verify that a private key matches its Certificate?*
- *Why do connections fail with an "alert bad certificate" error?*
- *Why does my 2048-bit private key not work?*
- *Why is client authentication broken after upgrading from SSLeay version 0.8 to 0.9?*
- *How can I convert a certificate from PEM to DER format?*
- *Why can't I find the `getca` or `getverisign` programs mentioned by Verisign, for installing my Verisign certificate?*
- *Can I use the Server Gated Cryptography (SGC) facility (aka Verisign Global ID) with mod_ssl?*
- *Why do browsers complain that they cannot verify my Verisign Global ID server certificate?*

What are RSA Private Keys, CSRs and Certificates?

An RSA private key file is a digital file that you can use to decrypt messages sent to you. It has a public component which you distribute (via your Certificate file) which allows people to encrypt those messages to you.

A Certificate Signing Request (CSR) is a digital file which contains your public key and your name. You send the CSR to a Certifying Authority (CA), who will convert it into a real Certificate, by signing it.

A Certificate contains your RSA public key, your name, the name of the CA, and is digitally signed by the CA. Browsers that know the CA can verify the signature on that Certificate, thereby obtaining your RSA public key. That enables them to send messages which only you can decrypt.

See the *Introduction* chapter for a general description of the SSL protocol.

Is there a difference on startup between a non-SSL-aware Apache and an SSL-aware Apache?

Yes. In general, starting Apache with `mod_ssl` built-in is just like starting Apache without it. However, if you have a passphrase on your SSL private key file, a startup dialog will pop up which asks you to enter the pass phrase.

Having to manually enter the passphrase when starting the server can be problematic - for example, when starting the server from the system boot scripts. In this case, you can follow the steps *below* to remove the passphrase from your private key. Bear in mind that doing so brings additional security risks - proceed with caution!

How do I create a self-signed SSL Certificate for testing purposes?

1. Make sure OpenSSL is installed and in your PATH.
2. Run the following command, to create `server.key` and `server.crt` files:
    ```
    $ openssl req -new -x509 -nodes -out server.crt -keyout server.key
    ```
    These can be used as follows in your `httpd.conf` file:
    ```
    SSLCertificateFile    /path/to/this/server.crt
    SSLCertificateKeyFile /path/to/this/server.key
    ```
3. It is important that you are aware that this `server.key` does *not* have any passphrase. To add a passphrase to the key, you should run the following command, and enter & verify the passphrase as requested.
    ```
    $ openssl rsa -des3 -in server.key -out server.key.new
    $ mv server.key.new server.key
    ```
    Please backup the `server.key` file, and the passphrase you entered, in a secure location.

How do I create a real SSL Certificate?

Here is a step-by-step description:

1. Make sure OpenSSL is installed and in your PATH.

    Create a RSA private key for your Apache server (will be Triple-DES encrypted and PEM formatted):

    ```
    $ openssl genrsa -des3 -out server.key 1024
    ```

    Please backup this server.key file and the pass-phrase you entered in a secure location. You can see the details of this RSA private key by using the command:

    ```
    $ openssl rsa -noout -text -in server.key
    ```

    If necessary, you can also create a decrypted PEM version (not recommended) of this RSA private key with:

    ```
    $ openssl rsa -in server.key -out server.key.unsecure
    ```

2. Create a Certificate Signing Request (CSR) with the server RSA private key (output will be PEM formatted):

    ```
    $ openssl req -new -key server.key -out server.csr
    ```

    Make sure you enter the FQDN ("Fully Qualified Domain Name") of the server when OpenSSL prompts you for the "CommonName", i.e. when you generate a CSR for a website which will be later accessed via https://www.foo.dom/, enter "www.foo.dom" here. You can see the details of this CSR by using

    ```
    $ openssl req -noout -text -in server.csr
    ```

3. You now have to send this Certificate Signing Request (CSR) to a Certifying Authority (CA) to be signed. Once the CSR has been signed, you will have a real Certificate, which can be used by Apache. You can have a CSR signed by a commercial CA, or you can create your own CA to sign it.
    Commercial CAs usually ask you to post the CSR into a web form, pay for the signing, and then send a signed Certificate, which you can store in a server.crt file. For more information about commercial CAs see the following locations:

    1. Verisign
        http://digitalid.verisign.com/server/apacheNotice.htm

    2. Thawte
        http://www.thawte.com/

    3. CertiSign Certificadora Digital Ltda.
        http://www.certisign.com.br

4. IKS GmbH
   http://www.iks-jena.de/leistungen/ca/

5. Uptime Commerce Ltd.
   http://www.uptimecommerce.com

6. BelSign NV/SA
   http://www.belsign.be

For details on how to create your own CA, and use this to sign a CSR, see below. Once your CSR has been signed, you can see the details of the Certificate as follows:

```
$ openssl x509 -noout -text -in server.crt
```

4. You should now have two files: `server.key` and `server.crt`. These can be used as follows in your `httpd.conf` file:

```
SSLCertificateFile     /path/to/this/server.crt
SSLCertificateKeyFile /path/to/this/server.key
```

The `server.csr` file is no longer needed.

How do I create and use my own Certificate Authority (CA)?

The short answer is to use the `CA.sh` or `CA.pl` script provided by OpenSSL. Unless you have a good reason not to, you should use these for preference. If you cannot, you can create a self-signed Certificate as follows:

1. Create a RSA private key for your server (will be Triple-DES encrypted and PEM formatted):

```
$ openssl genrsa -des3 -out server.key 1024
```

Please backup this `host.key` file and the pass-phrase you entered in a secure location. You can see the details of this RSA private key by using the command:

```
$ openssl rsa -noout -text -in server.key
```

If necessary, you can also create a decrypted PEM version (not recommended) of this RSA private key with:

```
$ openssl rsa -in server.key -out server.key.unsecure
```

2. Create a self-signed Certificate (X509 structure) with the RSA key you just created (output will be PEM formatted):

```
$ openssl req -new -x509 -nodes -sha1 -days 365 -key server.key -out
server.crt
```

This signs the server CSR and results in a `server.crt` file.
You can see the details of this Certificate using:

```
$ openssl x509 -noout -text -in server.crt
```

How can I change the pass-phrase on my private key file?

You simply have to read it with the old pass-phrase and write it again, specifying the new pass-phrase. You can accomplish this with the following commands:

```
$ openssl rsa -des3 -in server.key -out server.key.new
$ mv server.key.new server.key
```

The first time you're asked for a PEM pass-phrase, you should enter the old pass-phrase. After that, you'll be asked again to enter a pass-phrase - this time, use the new pass-phrase. If you are asked to verify the pass-phrase, you'll need to enter the new pass-phrase a second time.

How can I get rid of the pass-phrase dialog at Apache startup time?

The reason this dialog pops up at startup and every re-start is that the RSA private key inside your server.key file is stored in encrypted format for security reasons. The pass-phrase is needed to decrypt this file, so it can be read and parsed. Removing the pass-phrase removes a layer of security from your server - proceed with caution!

1. Remove the encryption from the RSA private key (while keeping a backup copy of the original file):

    ```
    $ cp server.key server.key.org
    $ openssl rsa -in server.key.org -out server.key
    ```

2. Make sure the server.key file is only readable by root:

    ```
    $ chmod 400 server.key
    ```

Now `server.key` contains an unencrypted copy of the key. If you point your server at this file, it will not prompt you for a pass-phrase. HOWEVER, if anyone gets this key they will be able to impersonate you on the net. PLEASE make sure that the permissions on this file are such that only root or the web server user can read it (preferably get your web server to start as root but run as another user, and have the key readable only by root).

As an alternative approach you can use the "`SSLPassPhraseDialog exec:/path/to/program`" facility. Bear in mind that this is neither more nor less secure, of course.

How do I verify that a private key matches its Certificate?

A private key contains a series of numbers. Two of these numbers form the "public key", the others are part of the "private key". The "public key" bits are included when you generate a CSR, and subsequently form part of the associated Certificate.

To check that the public key in your Certificate matches the public portion of your private key, you simply need to compare these numbers. To view the Certificate and the key run the commands:

```
$ openssl x509 -noout -text -in server.crt
$ openssl rsa -noout -text -in server.key
```

The `modulus' and the `public exponent' portions in the key and the Certificate must match. As the public exponent is usually 65537 and it's difficult to visually check that the long modulus numbers are the same, you can use the following approach:

```
$ openssl x509 -noout -modulus -in server.crt | openssl md5
$ openssl rsa -noout -modulus -in server.key | openssl md5
```

This leaves you with two rather shorter numbers to compare. It is, in theory, possible that these numbers may be the same, without the modulus numbers being the same, but the chances of this are overwhelmingly remote.

Should you wish to check to which key or certificate a particular CSR belongs you can perform the same calculation on the CSR as follows:

```
$ openssl req -noout -modulus -in server.csr | openssl md5
```

Why do connections fail with an "alert bad certificate" error?

Errors such as OpenSSL: error:14094412: SSL routines:SSL3_READ_BYTES:sslv3 alert bad certificate in the SSL logfile, are usually caused by a browser which is unable to handle the server certificate/private-key. For example, Netscape Navigator 3.x is unable to handle RSA key lengths not equal to 1024 bits.

Why does my 2048-bit private key not work?

The private key sizes for SSL must be either 512 or 1024 bits, for compatibility with certain web browsers. A keysize of 1024 bits is recommended because keys larger than 1024 bits are incompatible with some versions of Netscape Navigator and Microsoft Internet Explorer, and with other browsers that use RSA's BSAFE cryptography toolkit.

Why is client authentication broken after upgrading from SSLeay version 0.8 to 0.9?

The CA certificates under the path you configured with SSLCACertificatePath are found by SSLeay through hash symlinks. These hash values are generated by the `openssl x509 -noout -hash' command. However, the algorithm used to calculate the hash for a certificate changed between SSLeay 0.8 and 0.9. You will need to remove all old hash symlinks and create new ones after upgrading. Use the Makefile provided by mod_ssl.

How can I convert a certificate from PEM to DER format?

The default certificate format for SSLeay/OpenSSL is PEM, which is simply Base64 encoded DER, with header and footer lines. For some applications (e.g. Microsoft Internet Explorer) you need the certificate in plain DER format. You can convert a PEM file `cert.pem` into the corresponding DER file `cert.der` using the following command: **$ openssl x509 -in cert.pem -out cert.der -outform DER**

Why can't I find the `getca` or `getverisign` programs mentioned by Verisign, for installing my Verisign certificate?

Verisign has never provided specific instructions for Apache+mod_ssl. The instructions provided are for C2Net's Stronghold (a commercial Apache based server with SSL support).

To install your certificate, all you need to do is to save the certificate to a file, and give the name of that file to the <u>SSLCertificateFile</u> directive. You will also need to give it the key file. For more information, see the <u>SSLCertificateKeyFile</u> directive.

Can I use the Server Gated Cryptography (SGC) facility (aka Verisign Global ID) with mod_ssl?

Yes. <u>mod_ssl</u> has included support for the SGC facility since version 2.1. No special configuration is required - just use the Global ID as your server certificate. The *step up* of the clients is then automatically handled by <u>mod_ssl</u> at run-time.

Why do browsers complain that they cannot verify my Verisign Global ID server certificate?

Verisign uses an intermediate CA certificate between the root CA certificate (which is installed in the browsers) and the server certificate (which you installed on the server). You should have received this additional CA certificate from Verisign. If not, complain to them. Then, configure this certificate with the <u>SSLCertificateChainFile</u> directive. This ensures that the intermediate CA certificate is sent to the browser, filling the gap in the certificate chain.

42.5. The SSL Protocol

- *Why do I get lots of random SSL protocol errors under heavy server load?*
- *Why does my webserver have a higher load, now that it serves SSL encrypted traffic?*
- *Why do HTTPS connections to my server sometimes take up to 30 seconds to establish a connection?*
- *What SSL Ciphers are supported by mod_ssl?*

- *Why do I get "no shared cipher" errors, when trying to use Anonymous Diffie-Hellman (ADH) ciphers?*
- *Why do I get a 'no shared ciphers' error when connecting to my newly installed server?*
- *Why can't I use SSL with name-based/non-IP-based virtual hosts?*
- *Is it possible to use Name-Based Virtual Hosting to identify different SSL virtual hosts?*
- *How do I get SSL compression working?*
- *When I use Basic Authentication over HTTPS the lock icon in Netscape browsers stays unlocked when the dialog pops up. Does this mean the username/password is being sent unencrypted?*
- *Why do I get I/O errors when connecting via HTTPS to an Apache+mod_ssl server with Microsoft Internet Explorer (MSIE)?*
- *Why do I get I/O errors, or the message "Netscape has encountered bad data from the server", when connecting via HTTPS to an Apache+mod_ssl server with Netscape Navigator?*

Why do I get lots of random SSL protocol errors under heavy server load?

There can be a number of reasons for this, but the main one is problems with the SSL session Cache specified by the SSLSessionCache directive. The DBM session cache is the most likely source of the problem, so using the SHM session cache (or no cache at all) may help.

Why does my webserver have a higher load, now that it serves SSL encrypted traffic?

SSL uses strong cryptographic encryption, which necessitates a lot of number crunching. When you request a webpage via HTTPS, everything (even the images) is encrypted before it is transferred. So increased HTTPS traffic leads to load increases.

Why do HTTPS connections to my server sometimes take up to 30 seconds to establish a connection?

This is usually caused by a /dev/random device for SSLRandomSeed which blocks the read(2) call until enough entropy is available to service the request. More information is available in the reference manual for the SSLRandomSeed directive.

What SSL Ciphers are supported by mod_ssl?

Usually, any SSL ciphers supported by the version of OpenSSL in use, are also supported by mod_ssl. Which ciphers are available can depend on the way you built OpenSSL. Typically, at least the following ciphers are supported:

1. RC4 with MD5
2. RC4 with MD5 (export version restricted to 40-bit key)
3. RC2 with MD5
4. RC2 with MD5 (export version restricted to 40-bit key)
5. IDEA with MD5
6. DES with MD5
7. Triple-DES with MD5

To determine the actual list of ciphers available, you should run the following:

```
$ openssl ciphers -v
```

Why do I get "no shared cipher" errors, when trying to use Anonymous Diffie-Hellman (ADH) ciphers?

By default, OpenSSL does *not* allow ADH ciphers, for security reasons. Please be sure you are aware of the potential side-effects if you choose to enable these ciphers.

In order to use Anonymous Diffie-Hellman (ADH) ciphers, you must build OpenSSL with "-DSSL_ALLOW_ADH", and then add "ADH" into your SSLCipherSuite.

Why do I get a 'no shared ciphers' error when connecting to my newly installed server?

Either you have made a mistake with your SSLCipherSuite directive (compare it with the pre-configured example in httpd.conf-dist) or you chose to use DSA/DH algorithms instead of RSA when you generated your private key and ignored or overlooked the warnings. If you have chosen DSA/DH, then your server cannot communicate using RSA-based SSL ciphers (at least until you configure an additional RSA-based certificate/key pair). Modern browsers like NS or IE can only communicate over SSL using RSA ciphers. The result is the "no shared ciphers" error. To fix this, regenerate your server certificate/key pair, using the RSA algorithm.

Why can't I use SSL with name-based/non-IP-based virtual hosts?

The reason is very technical, and a somewhat "chicken and egg" problem. The SSL protocol layer stays below the HTTP protocol layer and encapsulates HTTP. When an SSL connection (HTTPS) is established Apache/mod_ssl has to negotiate the SSL protocol parameters with the client. For this, mod_ssl has to consult the configuration of the virtual server (for instance it has to look for the cipher suite, the server certificate, etc.). But in order to go to the correct virtual server Apache has to know the Host HTTP header field. To do this, the HTTP request header has to be read. This cannot be done before the SSL handshake is finished, but the information is needed in order to complete the SSL handshake phase. Bingo!

Why is it not possible to use Name-Based Virtual Hosting to identify different SSL virtual hosts?

Name-Based Virtual Hosting is a very popular method of identifying different virtual hosts. It allows you to use the same IP address and the same port number for many different sites. When people move on to SSL, it seems natural to assume that the same method can be used to have lots of different SSL virtual hosts on the same server.

It is possible, but only if using a 2.2.12 or later web server, built with 0.9.8j or later OpenSSL. This is because it requires a feature that only the most recent revisions of the SSL specification added, called Server Name Indication (SNI).

The reason is that the SSL protocol is a separate layer which encapsulates the HTTP protocol. So the SSL session is a separate transaction, that takes place before the HTTP session has begun. The server receives an SSL request on IP address X and port Y (usually 443). Since the SSL request did not contain any Host: field, the server had no way to decide which SSL virtual host to use. Usually, it just used the first one it found which matched the port and IP address specified.

If you are using a version of the web server and OpenSSL that support SNI, though, and the client's browser also supports SNI, then the hostname is included in the original SSL request, and the web server can select the correct SSL virtual host.

You can, of course, use Name-Based Virtual Hosting to identify many non-SSL virtual hosts (all on port 80, for example) and then have a single SSL virtual host (on port 443). But if you do this, you must make sure to put the non-SSL port number on the NameVirtualHost directive, e.g.

```
NameVirtualHost 192.168.1.1:80
```

Other workaround solutions include:

Using separate IP addresses for different SSL hosts. Using different port numbers for different SSL hosts.

How do I get SSL compression working?

Although SSL compression negotiation was defined in the specification of SSLv2 and TLS, it took until May 2004 for RFC 3749 to define DEFLATE as a negotiable standard compression method.

OpenSSL 0.9.8 started to support this by default when compiled with the zlib option. If both the client and the server support compression, it will be used. However, most clients still try to initially connect with an SSLv2 Hello. As SSLv2 did not include an array of prefered compression algorithms in its handshake, compression cannot be negotiated with these clients. If the client disables support for SSLv2, either an SSLv3 or TLS Hello may be sent, depending on which SSL library is used, and compression may be set up. You can verify whether clients make use of SSL compression by logging the %{SSL_COMPRESS_METHOD}x variable.

When I use Basic Authentication over HTTPS the lock icon in Netscape browsers stays unlocked when the dialog pops up. Does this mean the username/password is being sent unencrypted?

No, the username/password is transmitted encrypted. The icon in Netscape browsers is not actually synchronized with the SSL/TLS layer. It only toggles to the locked state when the first part of the actual webpage data is transferred, which may confuse people. The Basic Authentication facility is part of the HTTP layer, which is above the SSL/TLS layer in HTTPS. Before any HTTP data communication takes place in HTTPS, the SSL/TLS layer has already completed its handshake phase, and switched to encrypted communication. So don't be confused by this icon.

Why do I get I/O errors when connecting via HTTPS to an Apache+mod_ssl server with Microsoft Internet Explorer (MSIE)?

The first reason is that the SSL implementation in some MSIE versions has some subtle bugs related to the HTTP keep-alive facility and the SSL close notify alerts on socket connection close. Additionally the interaction between SSL and HTTP/1.1 features are problematic in some MSIE versions. You can work around these problems by forcing Apache not to use HTTP/1.1, keep-alive connections or send the SSL close notify messages to MSIE clients. This can be done by using the following directive in your SSL-aware virtual host section:

```
SetEnvIf User-Agent ".*MSIE.*" \
nokeepalive ssl-unclean-shutdown \
downgrade-1.0 force-response-1.0
```

Further, some MSIE versions have problems with particular ciphers. Unfortunately, it is not possible to implement a MSIE-specific workaround for this, because the ciphers are needed as early as the SSL handshake phase. So a MSIE-specific SetEnvIf won't solve these problems. Instead, you will have to make more drastic adjustments to the global parameters. Before you decide to do this, make sure your clients really have problems. If not, do not make these changes - they will affect *all* your clients, MSIE or otherwise.

The next problem is that 56bit export versions of MSIE 5.x browsers have a broken SSLv3 implementation, which interacts badly with OpenSSL versions greater than 0.9.4. You can accept this and require your clients to upgrade their browsers, you can downgrade to OpenSSL 0.9.4 (not advised), or you can work around this, accepting that your workaround will affect other browsers too:

```
SSLProtocol all -SSLv3
```

will completely disables the SSLv3 protocol and allow those browsers to work. A better workaround is to disable only those ciphers which cause trouble.

```
SSLCipherSuite ALL:!ADH:!EXPORT56:RC4+RSA:+HIGH:+MEDIUM:+LOW:+SSLv2:+EXP
```

This also allows the broken MSIE versions to work, but only removes the newer 56bit TLS ciphers.

Another problem with MSIE 5.x clients is that they refuse to connect to URLs of the form `https://12.34.56.78/` (where IP-addresses are used instead of the hostname), if the server is using the Server Gated Cryptography (SGC) facility. This can only be avoided by using the fully qualified domain name (FQDN) of the website in hyperlinks instead, because MSIE 5.x has an error in the way it handles the SGC negotiation.

And finally there are versions of MSIE which seem to require that an SSL session can be reused (a totally non standard-conforming behaviour, of course). Connecting with those MSIE versions only work if a SSL session cache is used. So, as a work-around, make sure you are using a session cache (see the SSLSessionCache directive).

Why do I get I/O errors, or the message "Netscape has encountered bad data from the server", when connecting via HTTPS to an Apache+mod_ssl server with Netscape Navigator?

This usually occurs when you have created a new server certificate for a given domain, but had previously told your browser to always accept the old server certificate. Once you clear the entry for the old certificate from your browser, everything should be fine. Netscape's SSL implementation is correct, so when you encounter I/O errors with Netscape Navigator it is usually caused by the configured certificates.

42.6. mod_ssl Support

- *What information resources are available in case of mod_ssl problems?*
- *What support contacts are available in case of mod_ssl problems?*
- *What information should I provide when writing a bug report?*
- *I had a core dump, can you help me?*
- *How do I get a backtrace, to help find the reason for my core dump?*

What information resources are available in case of mod_ssl problems?

The following information resources are available. In case of problems you should search here first.

Answers in the User Manual's F.A.Q. List (this)

http://httpd.apache.org/docs/2.2/ssl/ssl_faq.html
First check the F.A.Q. (this text). If your problem is a common one, it may have been answered several times before, and been included in this doc.

Postings from the modssl-users Support Mailing List *http://www.modssl.org/support/*

Search for your problem in the archives of the modssl-users mailing list. You're probably not the first person to have had this problem!

What support contacts are available in case of mod_ssl problems?

The following lists all support possibilities for mod_ssl, in order of preference. Please go through these possibilities *in this order* - don't just pick the one you like the look of.

1. *Send a Problem Report to the modssl-users Support Mailing List*
   modssl-users@modssl.org
   This is the preferred way of submitting your problem report, because this way, others can see the problem, and learn from any answers. You must subscribe to the list first, but you can then easily discuss your problem with both the author and the whole mod_ssl user community.

2. *Send a Problem Report to the Apache httpd Users Support Mailing List*
   users@httpd.apache.org
   This is the second way of submitting your problem report. Again, you must subscribe to the list first, but you can then easily discuss your problem with the whole Apache httpd user community.

3. *Write a Problem Report in the Bug Database*
   http://httpd.apache.org/bug_report.html
   This is the last way of submitting your problem report. You should only do this if you've already posted to the mailing lists, and had no success. Please follow the instructions on the above page *carefully*.

What information should I provide when writing a bug report?

You should always provide at least the following information:

Apache and OpenSSL version information

The Apache version can be determined by running `httpd -v`. The OpenSSL version can be determined by running `openssl version`. Alternatively, if you have Lynx installed, you can run the command `lynx -mime_header http://localhost/ | grep Server` to gather this information in a single step.

The details on how you built and installed Apache+mod_ssl+OpenSSL

For this you can provide a logfile of your terminal session which shows the configuration and install steps. If this is not possible, you should at least provide the `configure` command line you used.

In case of core dumps please include a Backtrace

If your Apache+mod_ssl+OpenSSL dumps its core, please attach a stack-frame "backtrace" (see below for information on how to get this). This information is required in order to find a reason for your core dump.

A detailed description of your problem

Don't laugh, we really mean it! Many problem reports don't include a description of what the actual problem is. Without this, it's very difficult for anyone to help you. So, it's in your own interest (you want the problem be solved, don't you?) to include as much detail as possible, please. Of course, you should still include all the essentials above too.

I had a core dump, can you help me?

In general no, at least not unless you provide more details about the code location where Apache dumped core. What is usually always required in order to help you is a backtrace (see next question). Without this information it is mostly impossible to find the problem and help you in fixing it.

How do I get a backtrace, to help find the reason for my core dump?

Following are the steps you will need to complete, to get a backtrace:

1. Make sure you have debugging symbols available, at least in Apache. On platforms where you use GCC/GDB, you will have to build Apache+mod_ssl with "OPTIM="-g -ggdb3"" to get this. On other platforms at least "OPTIM="-g"" is needed.

2. Start the server and try to reproduce the core-dump. For this you may want to use a directive like "CoreDumpDirectory /tmp" to make sure that the core-dump file can be written. This should result in a `/tmp/core` or `/tmp/httpd.core` file. If you don't get one of these, try running your server under a non-root UID. Many modern kernels do not allow a process to dump core after it has done a `setuid()` (unless it does an `exec()`) for security reasons (there can be privileged information left over in memory). If necessary, you can run `/path/to/httpd -X` manually to force Apache to not fork.

3. Analyze the core-dump. For this, run `gdb /path/to/httpd /tmp/httpd.core` or a similar command. In GDB, all you have to do then is to enter `bt`, and voila, you get the backtrace. For other debuggers consult your local debugger manual.

Part VI.

Guides, Tutorials, and HowTos

How-To / Tutorials

Authentication and Authorization

Authentication is any process by which you verify that someone is who they claim they are. Authorization is any process by which someone is allowed to be where they want to go, or to have information that they want to have.

See: *Authentication, Authorization*

Access Control

Access control refers to the process of restricting, or granting access to a resource based on arbitrary criteria. There are a variety of different ways that this can be accomplished.

See: *Access Control*

Dynamic Content with CGI

The CGI (Common Gateway Interface) defines a way for a web server to interact with external content-generating programs, which are often referred to as CGI programs or CGI scripts. It is the simplest, and most common, way to put dynamic content on your web site. This document will be an introduction to setting up CGI on your Apache web server, and getting started writing CGI programs.

See: *CGI: Dynamic Content*

.htaccess files

`.htaccess` files provide a way to make configuration changes on a per-directory basis. A file, containing one or more configuration directives, is placed in a particular document directory, and the directives apply to that directory, and all subdirectories thereof.

See: `.htaccess` *files*

Introduction to Server Side Includes

SSI (Server Side Includes) are directives that are placed in HTML pages, and evaluated on the server while the pages are being served. They let you add dynamically generated content to an existing HTML page, without having to serve the entire page via a CGI program, or other dynamic technology.

See: *Server Side Includes (SSI)*

Per-user web directories

On systems with multiple users, each user can be permitted to have a web site in their home directory using the `UserDir` directive. Visitors to a URL `http://example.com/~username/` will get content out of the home directory of the user "username", out of the subdirectory specified by the `UserDir` directive.

See: *User web directories (`public_html`)*

Chapter 43.

Authentication, Authorization and Access Control

Authentication is any process by which you verify that someone is who they claim they are. Authorization is any process by which someone is allowed to be where they want to go, or to have information that they want to have.

43.1. Related Modules and Directives

There are three types of modules involved in the authentication and authorization process. You will usually need to choose at least one module from each group.

- Authentication type (see the AuthType directive)
  - mod_auth_basic
  - mod_auth_digest
- Authentication provider
  - mod_authn_alias
  - mod_authn_anon
  - mod_authn_dbd
  - mod_authn_dbm
  - mod_authn_default
  - mod_authn_file
  - mod_authnz_ldap
- Authorization (see the Require directive)
  - mod_authnz_ldap
  - mod_authz_dbm
  - mod_authz_default
  - mod_authz_groupfile
  - mod_authz_owner
  - mod_authz_user

The module `mod_authnz_ldap` is both an authentication and authorization provider. The module `mod_authn_alias` is not an authentication provider in itself, but allows other authentication providers to be configured in a flexible manner.

The module `mod_authz_host` provides authorization and access control based on hostname, IP address or characteristics of the request, but is not part of the authentication provider system.

You probably also want to take a look at the *Access Control* howto, which discusses the various ways to control access to your server.

43.2. Introduction

If you have information on your web site that is sensitive or intended for only a small group of people, the techniques in this article will help you make sure that the people that see those pages are the people that you wanted to see them.

This article covers the "standard" way of protecting parts of your web site that most of you are going to use.

 Note

> If your data really needs to be secure, consider using `mod_ssl` in addition to any authentication.

43.3. The Prerequisites

The directives discussed in this article will need to go either in your main server configuration file (typically in a `<Directory>` section), or in per-directory configuration files (`.htaccess` files).

If you plan to use `.htaccess` files, you will need to have a server configuration that permits putting authentication directives in these files. This is done with the `AllowOverride` directive, which specifies which directives, if any, may be put in per-directory configuration files.

Since we're talking here about authentication, you will need an `AllowOverride` directive like the following:

```
AllowOverride AuthConfig
```

Or, if you are just going to put the directives directly in your main server configuration file, you will of course need to have write permission to that file.

And you'll need to know a little bit about the directory structure of your server, in order to know where some files are kept. This should not be terribly difficult, and I'll try to make this clear when we come to that point.

43.4. Getting it working

Here's the basics of password protecting a directory on your server.

First, you need to create a password file. Exactly how you do this will vary depending on what authentication provider you have chosen. More on that later. To start with, we'll use a text password file.

This file should be placed somewhere not accessible from the web. This is so that folks cannot download the password file. For example, if your documents are served out of /usr/local/apache/htdocs you might want to put the password file(s) in /usr/local/apache/passwd.

To create the file, use the *htpasswd* utility that came with Apache. This will be located in the bin directory of wherever you installed Apache. If you have installed Apache from a third-party package, it may be in your execution path.

To create the file, type:

```
htpasswd -c /usr/local/apache/passwd/passwords rbowen
```

htpasswd will ask you for the password, and then ask you to type it again to confirm it:

```
# htpasswd -c /usr/local/apache/passwd/passwords rbowen
New password: mypassword
Re-type new password: mypassword
Adding password for user rbowen
```

If *htpasswd* is not in your path, of course you'll have to type the full path to the file to get it to run. With a default installation, it's located at /usr/local/apache2/bin/htpasswd

Next, you'll need to configure the server to request a password and tell the server which users are allowed access. You can do this either by editing the httpd.conf file or using an .htaccess file. For example, if you wish to protect the directory /usr/local/apache/htdocs/secret, you can use the following directives, either placed in the file /usr/local/apache/htdocs/secret/.htaccess, or placed in httpd.conf inside a <Directory /usr/local/apache/apache/htdocs/secret> section.

```
AuthType Basic
AuthName "Restricted Files"
# (Following line optional)
AuthBasicProvider file
AuthUserFile /usr/local/apache/passwd/passwords
Require user rbowen
```

Let's examine each of those directives individually. The AuthType directive selects that method that is used to authenticate the user. The most common method is Basic, and this is the method implemented by mod_auth_basic. It is important to be aware, however, that Basic authentication sends the password from the client to the server unencrypted. This method should therefore not be used for highly sensitive data, unless accompanied by mod_ssl. Apache supports one other authentication method: AuthType Digest. This method is implemented by mod_auth_digest and is much more secure. Most recent browsers support Digest authentication.

The AuthName directive sets the *Realm* to be used in the authentication. The realm serves two major functions. First, the client often presents this information to the user as part of the password dialog box. Second, it is used by the client to determine what password to send for a given authenticated area.

So, for example, once a client has authenticated in the "Restricted Files" area, it will automatically retry the same password for any area on the same server that is marked with the "Restricted Files" Realm. Therefore, you can prevent a user from being prompted more than once for a password by letting multiple restricted areas share the same realm. Of course, for security reasons, the client will always need to ask again for the password whenever the hostname of the server changes.

The AuthBasicProvider is, in this case, optional, since file is the default value for this directive. You'll need to use this directive if you are choosing a different source for authentication, such as mod_authn_dbm or mod_authn_dbd.

The AuthUserFile directive sets the path to the password file that we just created with *htpasswd*. If you have a large number of users, it can be quite slow to search through a plain text file to authenticate the user on each request. Apache also has the ability to store user information in fast database files. The mod_authn_dbm module provides the AuthDBMUserFile directive. These files can be created and manipulated with the *dbmmanage* program. Many other types of authentication options are available from third party modules in the *Apache Modules Database*[1].

Finally, the Require directive provides the authorization part of the process by setting the user that is allowed to access this region of the server. In the next section, we discuss various ways to use the Require directive.

43.5. Letting more than one person in

The directives above only let one person (specifically someone with a username of rbowen) into the directory. In most cases, you'll want to let more than one person in. This is where the AuthGroupFile comes in.

---

[1] *http://modules.apache.org/*

If you want to let more than one person in, you'll need to create a group file that associates group names with a list of users in that group. The format of this file is pretty simple, and you can create it with your favorite editor. The contents of the file will look like this:

```
GroupName: rbowen dpitts sungo rshersey
```

That's just a list of the members of the group in a long line separated by spaces.

To add a user to your already existing password file, type:

```
htpasswd /usr/local/apache/passwd/passwords dpitts
```

You'll get the same response as before, but it will be appended to the existing file, rather than creating a new file. (It's the -c that makes it create a new password file).

Now, you need to modify your .htaccess file to look like the following:

```
AuthType Basic
AuthName "By Invitation Only"
# Optional line:
AuthBasicProvider file
AuthUserFile /usr/local/apache/passwd/passwords
AuthGroupFile /usr/local/apache/passwd/groups
Require group GroupName
```

Now, anyone that is listed in the group GroupName, and has an entry in the password file, will be let in, if they type the correct password.

There's another way to let multiple users in that is less specific. Rather than creating a group file, you can just use the following directive:

```
Require valid-user
```

Using that rather than the Require user rbowen line will allow anyone in that is listed in the password file, and who correctly enters their password. You can even emulate the group behavior here, by just keeping a separate password file for each group. The advantage of this approach is that Apache only has to check one file, rather than two. The disadvantage is that you have to maintain a bunch of password files, and remember to reference the right one in the AuthUserFile directive.

43.6. Possible problems

Because of the way that Basic authentication is specified, your username and password must be verified every time you request a document from the server. This is even if you're reloading the same page, and for every image on the page (if they come from a protected directory). As you can imagine, this slows things down a little. The amount that it slows things down is proportional to the size of the password file, because it has to open up that file, and go down the list of users until it gets to your name. And it has to do this every time a page is loaded.

A consequence of this is that there's a practical limit to how many users you can put in one password file. This limit will vary depending on the performance of your particular server machine, but you can expect to see slowdowns once you get above a few hundred entries, and may wish to consider a different authentication method at that time.

43.7. Alternate password storage

Because storing passwords in plain text files has the above problems, you may wish to store your passwords somewhere else, such as in a database.

mod_authn_dbm and mod_authn_dbd are two modules which make this possible. Rather than selecting AuthBasicProvider file, instead you can choose dbm or dbd as your storage format.

To select a dbd file rather than a text file, for example:

```
<Directory /www/docs/private>
AuthName "Private"
AuthType Basic
AuthBasicProvider dbm
AuthDBMUserFile /www/passwords/passwd.dbm
Require valid-user
</Directory>
```

Other options are available. Consult the mod_authn_dbm documentation for more details.

43.8. More information

You should also read the documentation for mod_auth_basic and mod_authz_host which contain some more information about how this all works. mod_authn_alias can also help in simplifying certain authentication configurations.

The various ciphers supported by Apache for authentication data are explained in *Password Encryptions*.

And you may want to look at the *Access Control* howto, which discusses a number of related topics.

Chapter 44.
Apache Tutorial: Dynamic Content with CGI

44.1. Introduction

Related Modules	Related Directives
mod_alias	AddHandler
mod_cgi	Options
	ScriptAlias

The CGI (Common Gateway Interface) defines a way for a web server to interact with external content-generating programs, which are often referred to as CGI programs or CGI scripts. It is the simplest, and most common, way to put dynamic content on your web site. This document will be an introduction to setting up CGI on your Apache web server, and getting started writing CGI programs.

44.2. Configuring Apache to permit CGI

In order to get your CGI programs to work properly, you'll need to have Apache configured to permit CGI execution. There are several ways to do this.

ScriptAlias

The `ScriptAlias` directive tells Apache that a particular directory is set aside for CGI programs. Apache will assume that every file in this directory is a CGI program, and will attempt to execute it, when that particular resource is requested by a client.

The `ScriptAlias` directive looks like:

```
ScriptAlias /cgi-bin/ /usr/local/apache2/cgi-bin/
```

The example shown is from your default `httpd.conf` configuration file, if you installed Apache in the default location. The `ScriptAlias` directive is much like the `Alias` directive, which defines a URL prefix that is to mapped to a particular directory. `Alias` and `ScriptAlias` are usually used for directories that are outside of the `DocumentRoot` directory. The difference between `Alias` and `ScriptAlias` is that `ScriptAlias` has the added meaning that everything under that URL prefix will be considered a CGI program.

So, the example above tells Apache that any request for a resource beginning with /cgi-bin/ should be served from the directory /usr/local/apache2/cgi-bin/, and should be treated as a CGI program.

For example, if the URL http://www.example.com/cgi-bin/test.pl is requested, Apache will attempt to execute the file /usr/local/apache2/cgi-bin/test.pl and return the output. Of course, the file will have to exist, and be executable, and return output in a particular way, or Apache will return an error message.

CGI outside of ScriptAlias directories

CGI programs are often restricted to ScriptAlias'ed directories for security reasons. In this way, administrators can tightly control who is allowed to use CGI programs. However, if the proper security precautions are taken, there is no reason why CGI programs cannot be run from arbitrary directories. For example, you may wish to let users have web content in their home directories with the UserDir directive. If they want to have their own CGI programs, but don't have access to the main cgi-bin directory, they will need to be able to run CGI programs elsewhere.

There are two steps to allowing CGI execution in an arbitrary directory. First, the cgi-script handler must be activated using the AddHandler or SetHandler directive. Second, ExecCGI must be specified in the Options directive.

Explicitly using Options to permit CGI execution

You could explicitly use the Options directive, inside your main server configuration file, to specify that CGI execution was permitted in a particular directory:

```
<Directory /usr/local/apache2/htdocs/somedir>
Options +ExecCGI
</Directory>
```

The above directive tells Apache to permit the execution of CGI files. You will also need to tell the server what files are CGI files. The following AddHandler directive tells the server to treat all files with the cgi or pl extension as CGI programs:

```
AddHandler cgi-script .cgi .pl
```

.htaccess files

The .htaccess *tutorial* shows how to activate CGI programs if you do not have access to httpd.conf.

User Directories

To allow CGI program execution for any file ending in .cgi in users' directories, you can use the following configuration.

```
<Directory /home/*/public_html>
Options +ExecCGI
AddHandler cgi-script .cgi
</Directory>
```

If you wish designate a `cgi-bin` subdirectory of a user's directory where everything will be treated as a CGI program, you can use the following.

```
<Directory /home/*/public_html/cgi-bin>
Options ExecCGI
SetHandler cgi-script
</Directory>
```

44.3. Writing a CGI program

There are two main differences between "regular" programming, and CGI programming.

First, all output from your CGI program must be preceded by a *MIME-type* header. This is HTTP header that tells the client what sort of content it is receiving. Most of the time, this will look like:

```
Content-type: text/html
```

Secondly, your output needs to be in HTML, or some other format that a browser will be able to display. Most of the time, this will be HTML, but occasionally you might write a CGI program that outputs a gif image, or other non-HTML content.

Apart from those two things, writing a CGI program will look a lot like any other program that you might write.

Your first CGI program

The following is an example CGI program that prints one line to your browser. Type in the following, save it to a file called `first.pl`, and put it in your `cgi-bin` directory.

```
#!/usr/bin/perl
print "Content-type: text/html\n\n";
print "Hello, World.";
```

Even if you are not familiar with Perl, you should be able to see what is happening here. The first line tells Apache (or whatever shell you happen to be running under) that this program can be executed by feeding the file to the interpreter found at the location `/usr/bin/perl`. The second line prints the content-type declaration we talked about, followed by two carriage-return newline pairs. This puts a blank line after the header, to indicate the end of the HTTP headers, and the beginning of the body. The third line prints the string "Hello, World.". And that's the end of it.

If you open your favorite browser and tell it to get the address

```
http://www.example.com/cgi-bin/first.pl
```

or wherever you put your file, you will see the one line `Hello, World.` appear in your browser window. It's not very exciting, but once you get that working, you'll have a good chance of getting just about anything working.

44.4. But it's still not working!

There are four basic things that you may see in your browser when you try to access your CGI program from the web:

The output of your CGI program

Great! That means everything worked fine. If the output is correct, but the browser is not processing it correctly, make sure you have the correct `Content-Type` set in your CGI program.

The source code of your CGI program or a "POST Method Not Allowed" message

That means that you have not properly configured Apache to process your CGI program. Reread the section on *configuring Apache* and try to find what you missed.

A message starting with "Forbidden"

That means that there is a permissions problem. Check the *Apache error log* and the section below on *file permissions*.

A message saying "Internal Server Error"

If you check the *Apache error log*, you will probably find that it says "Premature end of script headers", possibly along with an error message generated by your CGI program. In this case, you will want to check each of the below sections to see what might be preventing your CGI program from emitting the proper HTTP headers.

File permissions

Remember that the server does not run as you. That is, when the server starts up, it is running with the permissions of an unprivileged user - usually `nobody`, or `www` - and so it will need extra permissions to execute files that are owned by you. Usually, the way to give a file sufficient permissions to be executed by `nobody` is to give everyone execute permission on the file:

```
chmod a+x first.pl
```

Also, if your program reads from, or writes to, any other files, those files will need to have the correct permissions to permit this.

Path information and environment

When you run a program from your command line, you have certain information that is passed to the shell without you thinking about it. For example, you have a PATH, which tells the shell where it can look for files that you reference.

When a program runs through the web server as a CGI program, it may not have the same PATH. Any programs that you invoke in your CGI program (like sendmail, for example) will need to be specified by a full path, so that the shell can find them when it attempts to execute your CGI program.

A common manifestation of this is the path to the script interpreter (often perl) indicated in the first line of your CGI program, which will look something like:

```
#!/usr/bin/perl
```

Make sure that this is in fact the path to the interpreter.

In addition, if your CGI program depends on other *environment variables*, you will need to assure that those variables are passed by Apache.

Program errors

Most of the time when a CGI program fails, it's because of a problem with the program itself. This is particularly true once you get the hang of this CGI stuff, and no longer make the above two mistakes. The first thing to do is to make sure that your program runs from the command line before testing it via the web server. For example, try:

```
cd /usr/local/apache2/cgi-bin
./first.pl
```

(Do not call the perl interpreter. The shell and Apache should find the interpreter using the *path information* on the first line of the script.)

The first thing you see written by your program should be a set of HTTP headers, including the Content-Type, followed by a blank line. If you see anything else, Apache will return the Premature end of script headers error if you try to run it through the server. See *Writing a CGI program* above for more details.

Error logs

The error logs are your friend. Anything that goes wrong generates message in the error log. You should always look there first. If the place where you are hosting your web site does not permit you access to the error log, you should probably host your site somewhere else. Learn to read the error logs, and you'll find that almost all of your problems are quickly identified, and quickly solved.

Suexec

The *suexec* support program allows CGI programs to be run under different user permissions, depending on which virtual host or user home directory they are located in. Suexec has very strict permission checking, and any failure in that checking will result in your CGI programs failing with `Premature end of script headers`.

To check if you are using suexec, run `apachectl -V` and check for the location of `SUEXEC_BIN`. If Apache finds an *suexec* binary there on startup, suexec will be activated.

Unless you fully understand suexec, you should not be using it. To disable suexec, simply remove (or rename) the *suexec* binary pointed to by `SUEXEC_BIN` and then restart the server. If, after reading about *suexec*, you still wish to use it, then run `suexec -V` to find the location of the suexec log file, and use that log file to find what policy you are violating.

44.5. What's going on behind the scenes?

As you become more advanced in CGI programming, it will become useful to understand more about what's happening behind the scenes. Specifically, how the browser and server communicate with one another. Because although it's all very well to write a program that prints "Hello, World.", it's not particularly useful.

Environment variables

Environment variables are values that float around you as you use your computer. They are useful things like your path (where the computer searches for the actual file implementing a command when you type it), your username, your terminal type, and so on. For a full list of your normal, every day environment variables, type `env` at a command prompt.

During the CGI transaction, the server and the browser also set environment variables, so that they can communicate with one another. These are things like the browser type (Netscape, IE, Lynx), the server type (Apache, IIS, WebSite), the name of the CGI program that is being run, and so on.

These variables are available to the CGI programmer, and are half of the story of the client-server communication. The complete list of required variables is at *http://hoohoo.ncsa.uiuc.edu/cgi/env.html*.

This simple Perl CGI program will display all of the environment variables that are being passed around. Two similar programs are included in the `cgi-bin` directory of the Apache distribution. Note that some variables are required, while others are optional, so you may see some variables listed that were not in the official list. In addition, Apache provides many different ways for you to *add your own environment variables* to the basic ones provided by default.

```
#!/usr/bin/perl
print "Content-type: text/html\n\n";
foreach $key (keys %ENV) {
print "$key --> $ENV{$key}<br>";
}
```

STDIN and STDOUT

Other communication between the server and the client happens over standard input (STDIN) and standard output (STDOUT). In normal everyday context, STDIN means the keyboard, or a file that a program is given to act on, and STDOUT usually means the console or screen.

When you POST a web form to a CGI program, the data in that form is bundled up into a special format and gets delivered to your CGI program over STDIN. The program then can process that data as though it was coming in from the keyboard, or from a file

The "special format" is very simple. A field name and its value are joined together with an equals (=) sign, and pairs of values are joined together with an ampersand (&). Inconvenient characters like spaces, ampersands, and equals signs, are converted into their hex equivalent so that they don't gum up the works. The whole data string might look something like:

```
name=Rich%20Bowen&city=Lexington&state=KY&sidekick=Squirrel%20Monkey
```

You'll sometimes also see this type of string appended to a URL. When that is done, the server puts that string into the environment variable called QUERY_STRING. That's called a GET request. Your HTML form specifies whether a GET or a POST is used to deliver the data, by setting the METHOD attribute in the FORM tag.

Your program is then responsible for splitting that string up into useful information. Fortunately, there are libraries and modules available to help you process this data, as well as handle other of the aspects of your CGI program.

44.6. CGI modules/libraries

When you write CGI programs, you should consider using a code library, or module, to do most of the grunt work for you. This leads to fewer errors, and faster development.

If you're writing CGI programs in Perl, modules are available on CPAN[1]. The most popular module for this purpose is CGI.pm. You might also consider CGI::Lite, which implements a minimal set of functionality, which is all you need in most programs.

If you're writing CGI programs in C, there are a variety of options. One of these is the CGIC library, from *http://www.boutell.com/cgic/*.

---

[1] *http://www.cpan.org/*

44.7. For more information

There are a large number of CGI resources on the web. You can discuss CGI problems with other users on the Usenet group *comp.infosystems.www.authoring.cgi*. And the -servers mailing list from the HTML Writers Guild is a great source of answers to your questions. You can find out more at *http://www.hwg.org/lists/hwg-servers/*.

And, of course, you should probably read the CGI specification, which has all the details on the operation of CGI programs. You can find the original version at the *NCSA*[2] and there is an updated draft at the *Common Gateway Interface RFC project*[3].

When you post a question about a CGI problem that you're having, whether to a mailing list, or to a newsgroup, make sure you provide enough information about what happened, what you expected to happen, and how what actually happened was different, what server you're running, what language your CGI program was in, and, if possible, the offending code. This will make finding your problem much simpler.

Note that questions about CGI problems should **never** be posted to the Apache bug database unless you are sure you have found a problem in the Apache source code.

---

[2] *http://hoohoo.ncsa.uiuc.edu/cgi/interface.html*
[3] *http://www.w3.org/CGI/*

Chapter 45.

Apache Tutorial:

Introduction to Server Side Includes

Server-side includes provide a means to add dynamic content to existing HTML documents.

45.1. Introduction

Related Modules	Related Directives
mod_include	Options
mod_cgi	XBitHack
mod_expires	AddType
	SetOutputFilter
	BrowserMatchNoCase

This article deals with Server Side Includes, usually called simply SSI. In this article, I'll talk about configuring your server to permit SSI, and introduce some basic SSI techniques for adding dynamic content to your existing HTML pages.

In the latter part of the article, we'll talk about some of the somewhat more advanced things that can be done with SSI, such as conditional statements in your SSI directives.

45.2. What are SSI?

SSI (Server Side Includes) are directives that are placed in HTML pages, and evaluated on the server while the pages are being served. They let you add dynamically generated content to an existing HTML page, without having to serve the entire page via a CGI program, or other dynamic technology.

The decision of when to use SSI, and when to have your page entirely generated by some program, is usually a matter of how much of the page is static, and how much needs to be recalculated every time the page is served. SSI is a great way to add small pieces of information, such as the current time. But if a majority of your page is being generated at the time that it is served, you need to look for some other solution.

45.3. Configuring your server to permit SSI

To permit SSI on your server, you must have the following directive either in your
`httpd.conf` file, or in a `.htaccess` file:

```
Options +Includes
```

This tells Apache that you want to permit files to be parsed for SSI directives. Note that
most configurations contain multiple `Options` directives that can override each other. You
will probably need to apply the `Options` to the specific directory where you want SSI
enabled in order to assure that it gets evaluated last.

Not just any file is parsed for SSI directives. You have to tell Apache which files should be
parsed. There are two ways to do this. You can tell Apache to parse any file with a particular
file extension, such as `.shtml`, with the following directives:

```
AddType text/html .shtml
AddOutputFilter INCLUDES .shtml
```

One disadvantage to this approach is that if you wanted to add SSI directives to an existing
page, you would have to change the name of that page, and all links to that page, in order to
give it a `.shtml` extension, so that those directives would be executed.

The other method is to use the `XBitHack` directive:

```
XBitHack on
```

`XBitHack` tells Apache to parse files for SSI directives if they have the execute bit set. So, to
add SSI directives to an existing page, rather than having to change the file name, you
would just need to make the file executable using `chmod`.

```
chmod +x pagename.html
```

A brief comment about what not to do. You'll occasionally see people recommending that
you just tell Apache to parse all `.html` files for SSI, so that you don't have to mess with
`.shtml` file names. These folks have perhaps not heard about `XBitHack`. The thing to keep
in mind is that, by doing this, you're requiring that Apache read through every single file
that it sends out to clients, even if they don't contain any SSI directives. This can slow things
down quite a bit, and is not a good idea.

Of course, on Windows, there is no such thing as an execute bit to set, so that limits your
options a little.

In its default configuration, Apache does not send the last modified date or content length
HTTP headers on SSI pages, because these values are difficult to calculate for dynamic
content. This can prevent your document from being cached, and result in slower perceived
client performance. There are two ways to solve this:

1. Use the `XBitHack Full` configuration. This tells Apache to determine the last modified date by looking only at the date of the originally requested file, ignoring the modification date of any included files.

2. Use the directives provided by mod_expires to set an explicit expiration time on your files, thereby letting browsers and proxies know that it is acceptable to cache them.

45.4. Basic SSI directives

SSI directives have the following syntax:

```
<!--#element attribute=value attribute=value ... -->
```

It is formatted like an HTML comment, so if you don't have SSI correctly enabled, the browser will ignore it, but it will still be visible in the HTML source. If you have SSI correctly configured, the directive will be replaced with its results.

The element can be one of a number of things, and we'll talk some more about most of these in the next installment of this series. For now, here are some examples of what you can do with SSI

Today's date

```
<!--#echo var="DATE_LOCAL" -->
```

The `echo` element just spits out the value of a variable. There are a number of standard variables, which include the whole set of environment variables that are available to CGI programs. Also, you can define your own variables with the `set` element.

If you don't like the format in which the date gets printed, you can use the `config` element, with a `timefmt` attribute, to modify that formatting.

```
<!--#config timefmt="%A %B %d, %Y" -->
Today is <!--#echo var="DATE_LOCAL" -->
```

Modification date of the file

```
This document last modified <!--#flastmod file="index.html" -->
```

This element is also subject to `timefmt` format configurations.

Including the results of a CGI program

This is one of the more common uses of SSI - to output the results of a CGI program, such as everybody's favorite, a "hit counter."

```
<!--#include virtual="/cgi-bin/counter.pl" -->
```

45.5. Additional examples

Following are some specific examples of things you can do in your HTML documents with SSI.

When was this document modified?

Earlier, we mentioned that you could use SSI to inform the user when the document was most recently modified. However, the actual method for doing that was left somewhat in question. The following code, placed in your HTML document, will put such a time stamp on your page. Of course, you will have to have SSI correctly enabled, as discussed above.

```
<!--#config timefmt="%A %B %d, %Y" -->
This file last modified <!--#flastmod file="ssi.shtml" -->
```

Of course, you will need to replace the `ssi.shtml` with the actual name of the file that you're referring to. This can be inconvenient if you're just looking for a generic piece of code that you can paste into any file, so you probably want to use the `LAST_MODIFIED` variable instead:

```
<!--#config timefmt="%D" -->
This file last modified <!--#echo var="LAST_MODIFIED" -->
```

For more details on the `timefmt` format, go to your favorite search site and look for `strftime`. The syntax is the same.

Including a standard footer

If you are managing any site that is more than a few pages, you may find that making changes to all those pages can be a real pain, particularly if you are trying to maintain some kind of standard look across all those pages.

Using an include file for a header and/or a footer can reduce the burden of these updates. You just have to make one footer file, and then include it into each page with the `include` SSI command. The `include` element can determine what file to include with either the `file` attribute, or the `virtual` attribute. The `file` attribute is a file path, *relative to the current directory*. That means that it cannot be an absolute file path (starting with /), nor can it contain ../ as part of that path. The `virtual` attribute is probably more useful, and should specify a URL relative to the document being served. It can start with a /, but must be on the same server as the file being served.

```
<!--#include virtual="/footer.html" -->
```

I'll frequently combine the last two things, putting a `LAST_MODIFIED` directive inside a footer file to be included. SSI directives can be contained in the included file, and includes can be nested - that is, the included file can include another file, and so on.

45.6. What else can I config?

In addition to being able to `config` the time format, you can also `config` two other things.

Usually, when something goes wrong with your SSI directive, you get the message

```
[an error occurred while processing this directive]
```

If you want to change that message to something else, you can do so with the `errmsg` attribute to the `config` element:

```
<!--#config errmsg="[It appears that you don't know how to use SSI]" -->
```

Hopefully, end users will never see this message, because you will have resolved all the problems with your SSI directives before your site goes live. (Right?)

And you can `config` the format in which file sizes are returned with the `sizefmt` attribute. You can specify `bytes` for a full count in bytes, or `abbrev` for an abbreviated number in Kb or Mb, as appropriate.

45.7. Executing commands

I expect that I'll have an article some time in the coming months about using SSI with small CGI programs. For now, here's something else that you can do with the `exec` element. You can actually have SSI execute a command using the shell (`/bin/sh`, to be precise - or the DOS shell, if you're on Win32). The following, for example, will give you a directory listing.

```
<pre>
<!--#exec cmd="ls" -->
</pre>
```

or, on Windows

```
<pre>
<!--#exec cmd="dir" -->
</pre>
```

You might notice some strange formatting with this directive on Windows, because the output from `dir` contains the string "`<dir>`" in it, which confuses browsers.

Note that this feature is exceedingly dangerous, as it will execute whatever code happens to be embedded in the `exec` tag. If you have any situation where users can edit content on your web pages, such as with a "guestbook", for example, make sure that you have this feature disabled. You can allow SSI, but not the `exec` feature, with the `IncludesNOEXEC` argument to the `Options` directive.

45.8. Advanced SSI techniques

In addition to spitting out content, Apache SSI gives you the option of setting variables, and using those variables in comparisons and conditionals.

Caveat

Most of the features discussed in this article are only available to you if you are running Apache 1.2 or later. Of course, if you are not running Apache 1.2 or later, you need to upgrade immediately, if not sooner. Go on. Do it now. We'll wait.

Setting variables

Using the `set` directive, you can set variables for later use. We'll need this later in the discussion, so we'll talk about it here. The syntax of this is as follows:

```
<!--#set var="name" value="Rich" -->
```

In addition to merely setting values literally like that, you can use any other variable, including *environment variables* or the variables discussed above (like LAST_MODIFIED, for example) to give values to your variables. You will specify that something is a variable, rather than a literal string, by using the dollar sign ($) before the name of the variable.

```
<!--#set var="modified" value="$LAST_MODIFIED" -->
```

To put a literal dollar sign into the value of your variable, you need to escape the dollar sign with a backslash.

```
<!--#set var="cost" value="\$100" -->
```

Finally, if you want to put a variable in the midst of a longer string, and there's a chance that the name of the variable will run up against some other characters, and thus be confused with those characters, you can place the name of the variable in braces, to remove this confusion. (It's hard to come up with a really good example of this, but hopefully you'll get the point.)

```
<!--#set var="date" value="${DATE_LOCAL}_${DATE_GMT}" -->
```

Conditional expressions

Now that we have variables, and are able to set and compare their values, we can use them to express conditionals. This lets SSI be a tiny programming language of sorts. `mod_include` provides an `if`, `elif`, `else`, `endif` structure for building conditional statements. This allows you to effectively generate multiple logical pages out of one actual page.

The structure of this conditional construct is:

```
<!--#if expr="test_condition" -->
<!--#elif expr="test_condition" -->
<!--#else -->
<!--#endif -->
```

A *test_condition* can be any sort of logical comparison - either comparing values to one another, or testing the "truth" of a particular value. (A given string is true if it is nonempty.) For a full list of the comparison operators available to you, see the mod_include documentation. Here are some examples of how one might use this construct.

In your configuration file, you could put the following line:

```
BrowserMatchNoCase macintosh Mac
BrowserMatchNoCase MSIE InternetExplorer
```

This will set environment variables "Mac" and "InternetExplorer" to true, if the client is running Internet Explorer on a Macintosh.

Then, in your SSI-enabled document, you might do the following:

```
<!--#if expr="${Mac} && ${InternetExplorer}" -->
Apologetic text goes here
<!--#else -->
Cool JavaScript code goes here
<!--#endif -->
```

Not that I have anything against IE on Macs - I just struggled for a few hours last week trying to get some JavaScript working on IE on a Mac, when it was working everywhere else. The above was the interim workaround.

Any other variable (either ones that you define, or normal environment variables) can be used in conditional statements. With Apache's ability to set environment variables with the SetEnvIf directives, and other related directives, this functionality can let you do some pretty involved dynamic stuff without ever resorting to CGI.

45.9. Conclusion

SSI is certainly not a replacement for CGI, or other technologies used for generating dynamic web pages. But it is a great way to add small amounts of dynamic content to pages, without doing a lot of extra work.

Chapter 46.

Apache Tutorial: .htaccess files

`.htaccess` files provide a way to make configuration changes on a per-directory basis.

46.1..htaccess files

Related Modules	Related Directives
core	AccessFileName
mod_authn_file	AllowOverride
mod_authz_groupfile	Options
mod_cgi	AddHandler
mod_include	SetHandler
mod_mime	AuthType
	AuthName
	AuthUserFile
	AuthGroupFile
	Require

46.2. What they are/How to use them

`.htaccess` files (or "distributed configuration files") provide a way to make configuration changes on a per-directory basis. A file, containing one or more configuration directives, is placed in a particular document directory, and the directives apply to that directory, and all subdirectories thereof.

 Note

If you want to call your `.htaccess` file something else, you can change the name of the file using the `AccessFileName` directive. For example, if you would rather call the file `.config` then you can put the following in your server configuration file:

`AccessFileName .config`

In general, `.htaccess` files use the same syntax as the *main configuration files*. What you can put in these files is determined by the `AllowOverride` directive. This directive specifies, in categories, what directives will be honored if they are found in a `.htaccess` file. If a directive is permitted in a `.htaccess` file, the documentation for that directive will contain an Override section, specifying what value must be in `AllowOverride` in order for that directive to be permitted.

For example, if you look at the documentation for the `AddDefaultCharset` directive, you will find that it is permitted in `.htaccess` files. (See the Context line in the directive summary.) The *Override* line reads `FileInfo`. Thus, you must have at least `AllowOverride FileInfo` in order for this directive to be honored in `.htaccess` files.

Example:

Context:	server config, virtual host, directory, .htaccess
Override:	FileInfo

If you are unsure whether a particular directive is permitted in a `.htaccess` file, look at the documentation for that directive, and check the Context line for ".htaccess".

46.3. When (not) to use .htaccess files

In general, you should never use `.htaccess` files unless you don't have access to the main server configuration file. There is, for example, a prevailing misconception that user authentication should always be done in `.htaccess` files. This is simply not the case. You can put user authentication configurations in the main server configuration, and this is, in fact, the preferred way to do things.

`.htaccess` files should be used in a case where the content providers need to make configuration changes to the server on a per-directory basis, but do not have root access on the server system. In the event that the server administrator is not willing to make frequent configuration changes, it might be desirable to permit individual users to make these changes in `.htaccess` files for themselves. This is particularly true, for example, in cases where ISPs are hosting multiple user sites on a single machine, and want their users to be able to alter their configuration.

However, in general, use of `.htaccess` files should be avoided when possible. Any configuration that you would consider putting in a `.htaccess` file, can just as effectively be made in a `<Directory>` section in your main server configuration file.

There are two main reasons to avoid the use of `.htaccess` files.

The first of these is performance. When `AllowOverride` is set to allow the use of `.htaccess` files, Apache will look in every directory for `.htaccess` files. Thus, permitting `.htaccess` files causes a performance hit, whether or not you actually even use them! Also, the `.htaccess` file is loaded every time a document is requested.

Further note that Apache must look for `.htaccess` files in all higher-level directories, in order to have a full complement of directives that it must apply. (See section on *how directives are applied*.) Thus, if a file is requested out of a directory `/www/htdocs/example`, Apache must look for the following files:

```
/.htaccess
/www/.htaccess
/www/htdocs/.htaccess
/www/htdocs/example/.htaccess
```

And so, for each file access out of that directory, there are 4 additional file-system accesses, even if none of those files are present. (Note that this would only be the case if `.htaccess` files were enabled for `/`, which is not usually the case.)

The second consideration is one of security. You are permitting users to modify server configuration, which may result in changes over which you have no control. Carefully consider whether you want to give your users this privilege. Note also that giving users less privileges than they need will lead to additional technical support requests. Make sure you clearly tell your users what level of privileges you have given them. Specifying exactly what you have set `AllowOverride` to, and pointing them to the relevant documentation, will save yourself a lot of confusion later.

Note that it is completely equivalent to put a `.htaccess` file in a directory `/www/htdocs/example` containing a directive, and to put that same directive in a Directory section `<Directory /www/htdocs/example>` in your main server configuration:

`.htaccess` file in `/www/htdocs/example`:

Contents of .htaccess file in /www/htdocs/example

```
AddType text/example .exm
```

Section from your httpd.conf file

```
<Directory /www/htdocs/example>
AddType text/example .exm
</Directory>
```

However, putting this configuration in your server configuration file will result in less of a performance hit, as the configuration is loaded once when Apache starts, rather than every time a file is requested.

The use of `.htaccess` files can be disabled completely by setting the <u>AllowOverride</u> directive to `none`:

```
AllowOverride None
```

46.4. How directives are applied

The configuration directives found in a .htaccess file are applied to the directory in which the .htaccess file is found, and to all subdirectories thereof. However, it is important to also remember that there may have been .htaccess files in directories higher up. Directives are applied in the order that they are found. Therefore, a .htaccess file in a particular directory may override directives found in .htaccess files found higher up in the directory tree. And those, in turn, may have overridden directives found yet higher up, or in the main server configuration file itself.

Example:

In the directory /www/htdocs/example1 we have a .htaccess file containing the following:

```
Options +ExecCGI
```

(Note: you must have "AllowOverride Options" in effect to permit the use of the "Options" directive in .htaccess files.)

In the directory /www/htdocs/example1/example2 we have a .htaccess file containing:

```
Options Includes
```

Because of this second .htaccess file, in the directory /www/htdocs/example1/example2, CGI execution is not permitted, as only Options Includes is in effect, which completely overrides any earlier setting that may have been in place.

Merging of .htaccess with the main configuration files

As discussed in the documentation on *Configuration Sections*, .htaccess files can override the <Directory> sections for the corresponding directory, but will be overriden by other types of configuration sections from the main configuration files. This fact can be used to enforce certain configurations, even in the presence of a liberal AllowOverride setting. For example, to prevent script execution while allowing anything else to be set in .htaccess you can use:

```
<Directory />
Allowoverride All
</Directory>

<Location />
Options +IncludesNoExec -ExecCGI
</Location>
```

46.5. Authentication example

If you jumped directly to this part of the document to find out how to do authentication, it is important to note one thing. There is a common misconception that you are required to use .htaccess files in order to implement password authentication. This is not the case. Putting authentication directives in a <Directory> section, in your main server configuration file, is the preferred way to implement this, and .htaccess files should be used only if you don't have access to the main server configuration file. See *above* for a discussion of when you should and should not use .htaccess files.

Having said that, if you still think you need to use a .htaccess file, you may find that a configuration such as what follows may work for you.

.htaccess file contents:

```
AuthType Basic
AuthName "Password Required"
AuthUserFile /www/passwords/password.file
AuthGroupFile /www/passwords/group.file
Require Group admins
```

Note that AllowOverride AuthConfig must be in effect for these directives to have any effect.

Please see the *authentication tutorial* for a more complete discussion of authentication and authorization.

46.6. Server Side Includes example

Another common use of .htaccess files is to enable Server Side Includes for a particular directory. This may be done with the following configuration directives, placed in a .htaccess file in the desired directory:

```
Options +Includes
AddType text/html shtml
AddHandler server-parsed shtml
```

Note that AllowOverride Options and AllowOverride FileInfo must both be in effect for these directives to have any effect.

Please see the *SSI tutorial* for a more complete discussion of server-side includes.

46.7. CGI example

Finally, you may wish to use a .htaccess file to permit the execution of CGI programs in a particular directory. This may be implemented with the following configuration:

```
Options +ExecCGI
AddHandler cgi-script cgi pl
```

Alternately, if you wish to have all files in the given directory be considered to be CGI programs, this may be done with the following configuration:

```
Options +ExecCGI
SetHandler cgi-script
```

Note that `AllowOverride Options` and `AllowOverride FileInfo` must both be in effect for these directives to have any effect.

Please see the *CGI tutorial* for a more complete discussion of CGI programming and configuration.

46.8. Troubleshooting

When you put configuration directives in a `.htaccess` file, and you don't get the desired effect, there are a number of things that may be going wrong.

Most commonly, the problem is that <u>`AllowOverride`</u> is not set such that your configuration directives are being honored. Make sure that you don't have a `AllowOverride None` in effect for the file scope in question. A good test for this is to put garbage in your `.htaccess` file and reload. If a server error is not generated, then you almost certainly have `AllowOverride None` in effect.

If, on the other hand, you are getting server errors when trying to access documents, check your Apache error log. It will likely tell you that the directive used in your `.htaccess` file is not permitted. Alternately, it may tell you that you had a syntax error, which you will then need to fix.

Chapter 47.

Per-user web directories

On systems with multiple users, each user can be permitted to have a web site in their home directory using the `UserDir` directive. Visitors to a URL `http://example.com/~username/` will get content out of the home directory of the user "username", out of the subdirectory specified by the `UserDir` directive.

47.1. Per-user web directories

Related Modules	Related Directives
mod_userdir	UserDir DirectoryMatch AllowOverride

47.2. Setting the file path with UserDir

The `UserDir` directive specifies a directory out of which per-user content is loaded. This directive may take several different forms.

If a path is given which does not start with a leading slash, it is assumed to be a directory path relative to the home directory of the specified user. Given this configuration:

```
UserDir public_html
```

the URL `http://example.com/~rbowen/file.html` will be translated to the file path `/home/rbowen/public_html/file.html`

If a path is given starting with a slash, a directory path will be constructed using that path, plus the username specified. Given this configuration:

```
UserDir /var/html
```

the URL `http://example.com/~rbowen/file.html` will be translated to the file path `/var/html/rbowen/file.html`

If a path is provided which contains an asterisk (*), a path is used in which the asterisk is replaced with the username. Given this configuration:

```
UserDir /var/www/*/docs
```

the URL `http://example.com/~rbowen/file.html` will be translated to the file path `/var/www/rbowen/docs/file.html`

Multiple directories or directory paths can also be set.

```
UserDir public_html /var/html
```

For the URL `http://example.com/~rbowen/file.html`, Apache will search for `~rbowen`. If it isn't found, Apache will search for `rbowen` in `/var/html`. If found, the above URL will then be translated to the file path `/var/html/rbowen/file.html`

47.3. Redirecting to external URLs

The `UserDir` directive can be used to redirect user directory requests to external URLs.

```
UserDir http://example.org/users/*/
```

The above example will redirect a request for `http://example.com/~bob/abc.html` to `http://example.org/users/bob/abc.html`.

47.4. Restricting what users are permitted to use this feature

Using the syntax shown in the UserDir documentation, you can restrict what users are permitted to use this functionality:

```
UserDir disabled root jro fish
```

The configuration above will enable the feature for all users except for those listed in the `disabled` statement. You can, likewise, disable the feature for all but a few users by using a configuration like the following:

```
UserDir disabled
UserDir enabled rbowen krietz
```

See `UserDir` documentation for additional examples.

47.5. Enabling a cgi directory for each user

In order to give each user their own cgi-bin directory, you can use a `<Directory>` directive to make a particular subdirectory of a user's home directory cgi-enabled.

```
<Directory /home/*/public_html/cgi-bin/>
Options ExecCGI
SetHandler cgi-script
</Directory>
```

Then, presuming that `UserDir` is set to `public_html`, a cgi program `example.cgi` could be loaded from that directory as:

```
http://example.com/~rbowen/cgi-bin/example.cgi
```

47.6. Allowing users to alter configuration

If you want to allows users to modify the server configuration in their web space, they will need to use `.htaccess` files to make these changed. Ensure that you have set `AllowOverride` to a value sufficient for the directives that you want to permit the users to modify. See the *.htaccess tutorial* for additional details on how this works.

Chapter 48.
Access Control

Access control refers to any means of controlling access to any resource. This is separate from *authentication and authorization*.

48.1. Related Modules and Directives

Access control can be done by several different modules. The most important of these is `mod_authz_host`. Other modules discussed in this document include `mod_setenvif` and `mod_rewrite`.

48.2. Access control by host

If you wish to restrict access to portions of your site based on the host address of your visitors, this is most easily done using `mod_authz_host`.

The `Allow` and `Deny` directives let you allow and deny access based on the host name, or host address, of the machine requesting a document. The `Order` directive goes hand-in-hand with these two, and tells Apache in which order to apply the filters.

The usage of these directives is:

```
Allow from address
```

where *address* is an IP address (or a partial IP address) or a fully qualified domain name (or a partial domain name); you may provide multiple addresses or domain names, if desired.

For example, if you have someone spamming your message board, and you want to keep them out, you could do the following:

```
Deny from 10.252.46.165
```

Visitors coming from that address will not be able to see the content covered by this directive. If, instead, you have a machine name, rather than an IP address, you can use that.

```
Deny from host.example.com
```

And, if you'd like to block access from an entire domain, you can specify just part of an address or domain name:

```
Deny from 192.168.205
Deny from phishers.example.com moreidiots.example
Deny from ke
```

Using Order will let you be sure that you are actually restricting things to the group that you want to let in, by combining a Deny and an Allow directive:

```
Order deny,allow
Deny from all
Allow from dev.example.com
```

Listing just the Allow directive would not do what you want, because it will let folks from that host in, in addition to letting everyone in. What you want is to let *only* those folks in.

48.3. Access control by environment variable

mod_authz_host, in conjunction with mod_setenvif, can be used to restrict access to your website based on the value of arbitrary environment variables. This is done with the Allow from env= and Deny from env= syntax.

```
SetEnvIf User-Agent BadBot GoAway=1
Order allow,deny
Allow from all
Deny from env=GoAway
```

 Warning

Access control by User-Agent is an unreliable technique, since the User-Agent header can be set to anything at all, at the whim of the end user.

In the above example, the environment variable GoAway is set to 1 if the User-Agent matches the string BadBot. Then we deny access for any request when this variable is set. This blocks that particular user agent from the site.

An environment variable test can be negated using the =! syntax:

```
Allow from env=!GoAway
```

48.4. Access control with mod_rewrite

The [F] RewriteRule flag causes a 403 Forbidden response to be sent. Using this, you can deny access to a resource based on arbitrary criteria.

For example, if you wish to block access to a resource between 8pm and 6am, you can do this using mod_rewrite.

```
RewriteEngine On
RewriteCond %{TIME_HOUR} >20 [OR]
RewriteCond %{TIME_HOUR} <07
RewriteRule ^/fridge - [F]
```

This will return a 403 Forbidden response for any request after 8pm or before 7am. This technique can be used for any criteria that you wish to check. You can also redirect, or otherwise rewrite these requests, if that approach is preferred.

48.5. More information

You should also read the documentation for mod_auth_basic and mod_authz_host which contain some more information about how this all works. mod_authn_alias can also help in simplifying certain authentication configurations.

See the *Authentication and Authorization* howto.

Part VII.
Platform Specific Notes

Microsoft Windows

Using Apache

This document explains how to install, configure and run Apache 2.0 under Microsoft Windows.

See: *Using Apache with Microsoft Windows*

Compiling Apache

There are many important points before you begin compiling Apache. This document explain them.

See: *Compiling Apache for Microsoft Windows*

Other Platforms

Novell NetWare

This document explains how to install, configure and run Apache 2.0 under Novell NetWare 5.1 and above.

See: *Using Apache With Novell NetWare*

EBCDIC

Version 1.3 of the Apache HTTP Server is the first version which includes a port to a (non-ASCII) mainframe machine which uses the EBCDIC character set as its native codeset.

 Warning

This document has not been updated to take into account changes made in the 2.0 version of the Apache HTTP Server. Some of the information may still be relevant, but please use it with care.

See: *The Apache EBCDIC Port*

Chapter 49.

Using Apache HTTP Server on Microsoft Windows

This document explains how to install, configure and run Apache 2.2 under Microsoft Windows. If you have questions after reviewing the documentation (and any event and error logs), you should consult the peer-supported *users' mailing list*[1].

This document assumes that you are installing a binary distribution of Apache. If you want to compile Apache yourself (possibly to help with development or tracking down bugs), see *Compiling Apache for Microsoft Windows*.

49.1. Operating System Requirements

The primary Windows platform for running Apache 2.2 is Windows 2000 or later. The binary installer only works with the x86 family of processors, such as Intel and AMD processors. Always obtain and install the current service pack to avoid operating system bugs.

> Running Apache on Windows 9x is ignored by the developers, and is strongly discouraged. On Windows NT 4.0, installing Service Pack 6 is required. Apache HTTP Server versions later than 2.2 will not run on any operating system earlier than Windows 2000.

49.2. Downloading Apache for Windows

Information on the latest versions of Apache can be found on the web site of the Apache web server at *http://httpd.apache.org/download.cgi*. There you will find the current release, as well as more recent alpha or beta test versions, and a list of HTTP and FTP mirrors from which you can download the Apache web server. Please use a mirror near to you for a fast and reliable download.

For Windows installations you should download the version of Apache for Windows with the `.msi` extension. This is a single Microsoft Installer file, which contains a ready-to-run

---

[1] *http://httpd.apache.org/userslist.html*

build of Apache. There is a separate `.zip` file, which contains only the source code, see the summary above.

49.3. Installing Apache for Windows

You need Microsoft Installer 2.0 or above for the installation to work. For Windows NT 4.0 and 2000 refer to Microsoft's article *KB 292539*[2]. Windows XP and later do not require this update. The Windows 98/ME installer engine appears to no longer be available from Microsoft, and these instructions no longer detail such prerequisites.

Note that you cannot install two versions of Apache 2.2 on the same computer with the binary installer. You can, however, install a version of the 1.3 series **and** a version of the 2.2 series on the same computer without problems. If you need to have two different 2.2 versions on the same computer, you have to *compile and install Apache from the source*.

Run the Apache `.msi` file you downloaded above. The installation will ask you for these things:

1. **Network Domain.** Enter the DNS domain in which your server is or will be registered in. For example, if your server's full DNS name is `server.mydomain.net`, you would type `mydomain.net` here.

2. **Server Name.** Your server's full DNS name. From the example above, you would type `server.mydomain.net` here.

3. **Administrator's Email Address.** Enter the server administrator's or webmaster's email address here. This address will be displayed along with error messages to the client by default.

4. **For whom to install Apache** Select `for All Users, on Port 80, as a Service - Recommended` if you'd like your new Apache to listen at port 80 for incoming traffic. It will run as a service (that is, Apache will run even if no one is logged in on the server at the moment) Select `only for the Current User, on Port 8080, when started Manually` if you'd like to install Apache for your personal experimenting or if you already have another WWW server running on port 80.

5. **The installation type.** Select `Typical` for everything except the source code and libraries for module development. With `Custom` you can specify what to install. A full install will require about 13 megabytes of free disk space. This does *not* include the size of your web site(s).

6. **Where to install.** The default path is `C:\Program Files\Apache Software Foundation` under which a directory called `Apache2.2` will be created by default.

---

[2] *http://support.microsoft.com/kb/292539/*

During the installation, Apache will configure the files in the `conf` subdirectory to reflect the chosen installation directory. However, if any of the configuration files in this directory already exist, they will not be overwritten. Instead, the new copy of the corresponding file will be left with the extension `.default`. So, for example, if `conf\httpd.conf` already exists, it will be renamed as `conf\httpd.conf.default`. After the installation you should manually check to see what new settings are in the `.default` file, and if necessary, update your existing configuration file.

Also, if you already have a file called `htdocs\index.html`, it will not be overwritten (and no `index.html.default` will be installed either). This means it should be safe to install Apache over an existing installation, although you would have to stop the existing running server before doing the installation, and then start the new one after the installation is finished.

After installing Apache, you must edit the configuration files in the `conf` subdirectory as required. These files will be configured during the installation so that Apache is ready to be run from the directory it was installed into, with the documents server from the subdirectory `htdocs`. There are lots of other options which you should set before you really start using Apache. However, to get started quickly, the files should work as installed.

49.4. Customizing Apache for Windows

Apache is configured by the files in the `conf` subdirectory. These are the same files used to configure the Unix version, but there are a few different directives for Apache on Windows. See the *directive index* for all the available directives.

The main differences in Apache for Windows are:

- Because Apache for Windows is multithreaded, it does not use a separate process for each request, as Apache can on Unix. Instead there are usually only two Apache processes running: a parent process, and a child which handles the requests. Within the child process each request is handled by a separate thread.

  The process management directives are also different:

  `MaxRequestsPerChild`: Like the Unix directive, this controls how many requests (actually, connections) which a single child process will serve before exiting. However, unlike on Unix, a replacement process is not instantly available. Use the default `MaxRequestsPerChild 0`, unless instructed to change the behavior to overcome a memory leak in third party modules or in-process applications.

> **Warning: The server configuration file is reread when a new child process is started. If you have modified `httpd.conf`, the new child may not start or you may receive unexpected results.**

`ThreadsPerChild`: This directive is new. It tells the server how many threads it should use. This is the maximum number of connections the server can handle at once, so be sure to set this number high enough for your site if you get a lot of hits. The recommended default is `ThreadsPerChild 150`, but this must be adjusted to reflect the greatest anticipated number of simultanious connections to accept.

The directives that accept filenames as arguments must use Windows filenames instead of Unix ones. However, because Apache may interpret backslashes as an "escape character" sequence, you should consistently use forward slashes in path names, not backslashes. Drive letters can be used; if omitted, the drive of the SystemRoot directive (or -d command line option) becomes the default.

- While filenames are generally case-insensitive on Windows, URLs are still treated internally as case-sensitive before they are mapped to the filesystem. For example, the `<Location>`, `Alias`, and `ProxyPass` directives all use case-sensitive arguments. For this reason, it is particularly important to use the `<Directory>` directive when attempting to limit access to content in the filesystem, since this directive applies to any content in a directory, regardless of how it is accessed. If you wish to assure that only lowercase is used in URLs, you can use something like:

```
RewriteEngine On
RewriteMap lowercase int:tolower
RewriteCond %{REQUEST_URI} [A-Z]
RewriteRule (.*) ${lowercase:$1} [R,L]
```

- When running, Apache needs write access only to the logs directory and any configured cache directory tree. Due to the issue of case insensitive and short 8.3 format names, Apache must validate all path names given. This means that each directory which Apache evaluates, from the drive root up to the directory leaf, must have read, list and traverse directory permissions. If Apache2.2 is installed at C:\Program Files, then the root directory, Program Files and Apache2.2 must all be visible to Apache.

- Apache for Windows contains the ability to load modules at runtime, without recompiling the server. If Apache is compiled normally, it will install a number of optional modules in the `\Apache2.2\modules` directory. To activate these or other modules, the new `LoadModule` directive must be used. For example, to activate the status module, use the following (in addition to the status-activating directives in `access.conf`):

```
LoadModule status_module modules/mod_status.so
```

Information on *creating loadable modules* is also available.

- Apache can also load ISAPI (Internet Server Application Programming Interface) extensions such as those used by Microsoft IIS and other Windows servers. *More information is available.* Note that Apache **cannot** load ISAPI Filters, and ISAPI Handlers with some Microsoft feature extensions will not work.

- When running CGI scripts, the method Apache uses to find the interpreter for the script is configurable using the `ScriptInterpreterSource` directive.

- Since it is often difficult to manage files with names like `.htaccess` in Windows, you may find it useful to change the name of this per-directory configuration file using the `AccessFilename` directive.

- Any errors during Apache startup are logged into the Windows event log when running on Windows NT. This mechanism acts as a backup for those situations where Apache is not yet prepared to use the `error.log` file. You can review the Windows Applicat Event Log by using the Event Viewer, e.g. Start - Settings - Control Panel - Administrative Tools - Event Viewer.

49.5. Running Apache as a Service

You can install Apache as a service automatically during the installation. If you chose to install for all users, the installation will create an Apache service for you. If you specify to install for yourself only, you can manually register Apache as a service after the installation. You have to be a member of the Administrators group for the service installation to succeed.

Apache comes with a utility called the Apache Service Monitor. With it you can see and manage the state of all installed Apache services on any machine on your network. To be able to manage an Apache service with the monitor, you have to first install the service (either automatically via the installation or manually).

You can install Apache as a Windows NT service as follows from the command prompt at the Apache `bin` subdirectory:

```
httpd.exe -k install
```

If you need to specify the name of the service you want to install, use the following command. You have to do this if you have several different service installations of Apache on your computer.

```
httpd.exe -k install -n "MyServiceName"
```

If you need to have specifically named configuration files for different services, you must use this:

```
httpd.exe -k install -n "MyServiceName" -f "c:\files\my.conf"
```

If you use the first command without any special parameters except -k install, the service will be called Apache2.2 and the configuration will be assumed to be conf\httpd.conf.

Removing an Apache service is easy. Just use:

```
httpd.exe -k uninstall
```

The specific Apache service to be uninstalled can be specified by using:

```
httpd.exe -k uninstall -n "MyServiceName"
```

Normal starting, restarting and shutting down of an Apache service is usually done via the Apache Service Monitor, by using commands like NET START Apache2.2 and NET STOP Apache2.2 or via normal Windows service management. Before starting Apache as a service by any means, you should test the service's configuration file by using:

```
httpd.exe -n "MyServiceName" -t
```

You can control an Apache service by its command line switches, too. To start an installed Apache service you'll use this:

```
httpd.exe -k start
```

To stop an Apache service via the command line switches, use this:

```
httpd.exe -k stop
```

or

```
httpd.exe -k shutdown
```

You can also restart a running service and force it to reread its configuration file by using:

```
httpd.exe -k restart
```

By default, all Apache services are registered to run as the system user (the LocalSystem account). The LocalSystem account has no privileges to your network via any Windows-secured mechanism, including the file system, named pipes, DCOM, or secure RPC. It has, however, wide privileges locally.

Never grant any network privileges to the LocalSystem account! If you need Apache to be able to access network resources, create a separate account for Apache as noted below.

It is recommended that users create a separate account for running Apache service(s). If you have to access network resources via Apache, this is required.

1. Create a normal domain user account, and be sure to memorize its password.

---

2. Grant the newly-created user a privilege of `Log on as a service` and `Act as part of the operating system`. On Windows NT 4.0 these privileges are granted via User Manager for Domains, but on Windows 2000 and XP you probably want to use Group Policy for propagating these settings. You can also manually set these via the Local Security Policy MMC snap-in.

3. Confirm that the created account is a member of the Users group.

4. Grant the account read and execute (RX) rights to all document and script folders (`htdocs` and `cgi-bin` for example).

5. Grant the account change (RWXD) rights to the Apache `logs` directory.

6. Grant the account read and execute (RX) rights to the `httpd.exe` binary executable.

> It is usually a good practice to grant the user the Apache service runs as read and execute (RX) access to the whole Apache2.2 directory, except the `logs` subdirectory, where the user has to have at least change (RWXD) rights.

If you allow the account to log in as a user and as a service, then you can log on with that account and test that the account has the privileges to execute the scripts, read the web pages, and that you can start Apache in a console window. If this works, and you have followed the steps above, Apache should execute as a service with no problems.

> **Error code 2186** is a good indication that you need to review the "Log On As" configuration for the service, since Apache cannot access a required network resource. Also, pay close attention to the privileges of the user Apache is configured to run as.

When starting Apache as a service you may encounter an error message from the Windows Service Control Manager. For example, if you try to start Apache by using the Services applet in the Windows Control Panel, you may get the following message:

```
Could not start the Apache2.2 service on \\COMPUTER
Error 1067; The process terminated unexpectedly.
```

You will get this generic error if there is any problem with starting the Apache service. In order to see what is really causing the problem you should follow the instructions for Running Apache for Windows from the Command Prompt.

If you are having problems with the service, it is suggested you follow the instructions below to try starting httpd.exe from a console window, and work out the errors before struggling to start it as a service again.

49.6. Running Apache as a Console Application

Running Apache as a service is usually the recommended way to use it, but it is sometimes easier to work from the command line (on Windows 9x running Apache from the command line is the recommended way due to the lack of reliable service support.)

To run Apache from the command line as a console application, use the following command:

```
httpd.exe
```

Apache will execute, and will remain running until it is stopped by pressing Control-C.

You can also run Apache via the shortcut Start Apache in Console placed to Start Menu --> Programs --> Apache HTTP Server 2.2.xx --> Control Apache Server during the installation. This will open a console window and start Apache inside it. If you don't have Apache installed as a service, the window will remain visible until you stop Apache by pressing Control-C in the console window where Apache is running in. The server will exit in a few seconds. However, if you do have Apache installed as a service, the shortcut starts the service. If the Apache service is running already, the shortcut doesn't do anything.

You can tell a running Apache to stop by opening another console window and entering:

```
httpd.exe -k shutdown
```

This should be preferred over pressing Control-C because this lets Apache end any current operations and clean up gracefully.

You can also tell Apache to restart. This forces it to reread the configuration file. Any operations in progress are allowed to complete without interruption. To restart Apache, either press Control-Break in the console window you used for starting Apache, or enter

```
httpd.exe -k restart
```

in any other console window.

Note for people familiar with the Unix version of Apache: these commands provide a Windows equivalent to kill -TERM *pid* and kill -USR1 *pid*. The command line option used, -k, was chosen as a reminder of the kill command used on Unix.

If the Apache console window closes immediately or unexpectedly after startup, open the Command Prompt from the Start Menu --> Programs. Change to the folder to which you installed Apache, type the command httpd.exe, and read the error message. Then change to the logs folder, and review the error.log file for configuration mistakes. If you accepted the defaults when you installed Apache, the commands would be:

```
c:
cd "\Program Files\Apache Software Foundation\Apache2.2\bin"
httpd.exe
```

Then wait for Apache to stop, or press Control-C. Then enter the following:

```
cd ..\logs
more < error.log
```

When working with Apache it is important to know how it will find the configuration file. You can specify a configuration file on the command line in two ways:

- -f specifies an absolute or relative path to a particular configuration file:

```
httpd.exe -f "c:\my server files\anotherconfig.conf"
```

or

```
httpd.exe -f files\anotherconfig.conf
```

- -n specifies the installed Apache service whose configuration file is to be used:

```
httpd.exe -n "MyServiceName"
```

In both of these cases, the proper ServerRoot should be set in the configuration file.

If you don't specify a configuration file with -f or -n, Apache will use the file name compiled into the server, such as conf\httpd.conf. This built-in path is relative to the installation directory. You can verify the compiled file name from a value labelled as SERVER_CONFIG_FILE when invoking Apache with the -V switch, like this:

```
httpd.exe -V
```

Apache will then try to determine its ServerRoot by trying the following, in this order:

1. A ServerRoot directive via the -C command line switch.
2. The -d switch on the command line.
3. Current working directory.
4. A registry entry which was created if you did a binary installation.
5. The server root compiled into the server. This is /apache by default, you can verify it by using httpd.exe -V and looking for a value labelled as HTTPD_ROOT.

During the installation, a version-specific registry key is created in the Windows registry. The location of this key depends on the type of the installation. If you chose to install Apache for all users, the key is located under the HKEY_LOCAL_MACHINE hive, like this (the version numbers will of course vary between different versions of Apache:

```
HKEY_LOCAL_MACHINE\SOFTWARE\Apache Software Foundation\Apache\2.2.2
```

Correspondingly, if you chose to install Apache for the current user only, the key is located under the HKEY_CURRENT_USER hive, the contents of which are dependent of the user currently logged on:

```
HKEY_CURRENT_USER\SOFTWARE\Apache Software Foundation\Apache\2.2.2
```

This key is compiled into the server and can enable you to test new versions without affecting the current version. Of course, you must take care not to install the new version in the same directory as another version.

If you did not do a binary install, Apache will in some scenarios complain about the missing registry key. This warning can be ignored if the server was otherwise able to find its configuration file.

The value of this key is the `ServerRoot` directory which contains the `conf` subdirectory. When Apache starts it reads the `httpd.conf` file from that directory. If this file contains a `ServerRoot` directive which contains a different directory from the one obtained from the registry key above, Apache will forget the registry key and use the directory from the configuration file. If you copy the Apache directory or configuration files to a new location it is vital that you update the `ServerRoot` directive in the `httpd.conf` file to reflect the new location.

49.7. Testing the Installation

After starting Apache (either in a console window or as a service) it will be listening on port 80 (unless you changed the `Listen` directive in the configuration files or installed Apache only for the current user). To connect to the server and access the default page, launch a browser and enter this URL:

```
http://localhost/
```

Apache should respond with a welcome page and you should see "It Works!". If nothing happens or you get an error, look in the `error.log` file in the `logs` subdirectory. If your host is not connected to the net, or if you have serious problems with your DNS (Domain Name Service) configuration, you may have to use this URL:

```
http://127.0.0.1/
```

If you happen to be running Apache on an alternate port, you need to explicitly put that in the URL:

```
http://127.0.0.1:8080/
```

Once your basic installation is working, you should configure it properly by editing the files in the `conf` subdirectory. Again, if you change the configuration of the Windows NT service for Apache, first attempt to start it from the command line to make sure that the service starts with no errors.

Because Apache **cannot** share the same port with another TCP/IP application, you may need to stop, uninstall or reconfigure certain other services before running Apache. These conflicting services include other WWW servers, some firewall implementations, and even some client applications (such as Skype) which will use port 80 to attempt to bypass firewall issues.

Chapter 50.
Compiling Apache for Microsoft Windows

There are many important points before you begin compiling Apache. See *Using Apache with Microsoft Windows* before you begin.

50.1. Requirements

Compiling Apache requires the following environment to be properly installed:

- Disk Space

  Make sure you have at least 200 MB of free disk space available. After installation Apache requires approximately 80 MB of disk space, plus space for log and cache files, which can grow rapidly. The actual disk space requirements will vary considerably based on your chosen configuration and any third-party modules or libraries, especially when OpenSSL is also built. Because many files are text and very easily compressed, NTFS filesystem compression cuts these requirements in half.

- Appropriate Patches

  The httpd binary is built with the help of several patches to third party packages, which ensure the released code is buildable and debuggable. These patches are available and distributed from *http://www.apache.org/dist/httpd/binaries/win32/patches_applied/* and are recommended to be applied to obtain identical results as the "official" ASF distributed binaries.

- Microsoft Visual C++ 6.0 (Visual Studio 97) or later.

  Apache can be built using the command line tools, or from within the Visual Studio IDE Workbench. The command line build requires the environment to reflect the PATH, INCLUDE, LIB and other variables that can be configured with the vcvars32.bat script.

> You may want the Visual Studio Processor Pack for your older version of Visual Studio, or a full (not Express) version of newer Visual Studio editions, for the ml.exe assembler. This will allow you to build OpenSSL, if desired, using the more efficient assembly code implementation.

> Only the Microsoft compiler tool chain is actively supported by the active httpd contributors. Although the project regularly accepts patches to ensure MinGW and other alternative builds work and improve upon them, they are not actively maintained and are often broken in the course of normal development.

- Updated Microsoft Windows Platform SDK, February 2003 or later.

  An appropriate Windows Platform SDK is included by default in the full (not express/lite) versions of Visual C++ 7.1 (Visual Studio 2002) and later, these users can ignore these steps unless explicitly choosing a newer or different version of the Platform SDK.

  To use Visual C++ 6.0 or 7.0 (Studio 2000 .NET), the Platform SDK environment must be prepared using the setenv.bat script (installed by the Platform SDK) before starting the command line build or launching the msdev/devenv GUI environment. Installing the Platform SDK for Visual Studio Express versions (2003 and later) should adjust the default environment appropriately.

```
"c:\Program Files\Microsoft Visual Studio\VC98\Bin\VCVARS32"
"c:\Program Files\Platform SDK\setenv.bat"
```

- Perl and awk

  Several steps recommended here require a perl interpreter during the build preparation process, but it is otherwise not required.

  To install Apache within the build system, several files are modified using the awk.exe utility. awk was chosen since it is a very small download (compared with Perl or WSH/VB) and accomplishes the task of modifying configuration files upon installation. Brian Kernighan's *http://www.cs.princeton.edu/~bwk/btl.mirror/* site has a compiled native Win32 binary, *http://www.cs.princeton.edu/~bwk/btl.mirror/awk95.exe* which you must save with the name awk.exe (rather than awk95.exe).

> If awk.exe is not found, Makefile.win's install target will not perform substitutions in the installed .conf files. You must manually modify the installed .conf files to allow the server to start. Search and replace all "@token@" tags as appropriate.

> The Visual Studio IDE will only find awk.exe from the PATH, or executable path specified in the menu option Tools -> Options -> (Projects ->) Directories. Ensure awk.exe is in your system path.

> Also note that if you are using Cygwin tools (*http://www.cygwin.com/*) the awk utility is named gawk.exe and that the file awk.exe is really a symlink to the gawk.exe

> file. The Windows command shell does not recognize symlinks, and because of this building InstallBin will fail. A workaround is to delete awk.exe from the cygwin installation and copy gawk.exe to awk.exe. Also note the cygwin/mingw ports of gawk 3.0.x were buggy, please upgrade to 3.1.x before attempting to use any gawk port.

- [Optional] zlib library (for <u>mod_deflate</u>)

  Zlib must be installed into a srclib subdirectory named zlib. This must be built in-place. Zlib can be obtained from *http://www.zlib.net/* -- the <u>mod_deflate</u> is confirmed to work correctly with version 1.2.3.

```
nmake -f win32\Makefile.msc
nmake -f win32\Makefile.msc test
```

- [Optional] OpenSSL libraries (for <u>mod_ssl</u> and ab.exe with ssl support)

> The OpenSSL library is cryptographic software. The country in which you currently reside may have restrictions on the import, possession, use, and/or re-export to another country, of encryption software. BEFORE using any encryption software, please check your country's laws, regulations and policies concerning the import, possession, or use, and re-export of encryption software, to see if this is permitted. See *http://www.wassenaar.org/* for more information.

Configuring and building OpenSSL requires perl to be installed.

OpenSSL must be installed into a srclib subdirectory named openssl, obtained from *http://www.openssl.org/source/*, in order to compile <u>mod_ssl</u> or the abs.exe project, which is ab.c with SSL support enabled. To prepare OpenSSL to be linked to Apache mod_ssl or abs.exe, and disable patent encumbered features in OpenSSL, you might use the following build commands:

```
perl Configure no-rc5 no-idea enable-mdc2 enable-zlib VC-WIN32 -
Ipath/to/srclib/zlib -Lpath/to/srclib/zlib
ms\do_masm.bat
nmake -f ms\ntdll.mak
```

> It is not advisable to use zlib-dynamic, as that transfers the cost of deflating SSL streams to the first request which must load the zlib dll. Note the suggested patch enables the -L flag to work with windows builds, corrects the name of zdll.lib and ensures .pdb files are generated for troubleshooting. If the assembler is not installed, you would add no-asm above and use ms\do_ms.bat instead of the ms\do_masm.bat script.

- [Optional] Database libraries (for mod_dbd and mod_authn_dbm)

  The apr-util library exposes dbm (keyed database) and dbd (query oriented database) client functionality to the httpd server and its modules, such as authentication and authorization. The sdbm dbm and odbc dbd providers are compiled unconditionally.

  The dbd support includes the Oracle instantclient package, MySQL, PostgreSQL and sqlite. To build these all, for example, set up the LIB to include the library path, INCLUDE to include the headers path, and PATH to include the dll bin path of all four SDK's, and set the DBD_LIST environment variable to inform the build which client driver SDKs are installed correctly, e.g.;

  ```
  set DBD_LIST=sqlite3 pgsql oracle mysql
  ```

  Similarly, the dbm support can be extended with DBM_LIST to build a Berkeley DB provider (db) and/or gdbm provider, by similarly configuring LIB, INCLUDE and PATH first to ensure the client library libs and headers are available.

  ```
  set DBM_LIST=db gdbm
  ```

  > Depending on the choice of database distributions, it may be necessary to change the actual link target name (e.g. gdbm.lib vs. libgdb.lib) that are listed in the corresponding .dsp/.mak files within the directories srclib\apr-util\dbd or ...\dbm.

  See the README-win32.txt file for more hints on obtaining the various database driver SDKs.

50.2. Command-Line Build

Makefile.win is the top level Apache makefile. To compile Apache on Windows, simply use one of the following commands to build the release or debug flavor:

```
nmake /f Makefile.win _apacher

nmake /f Makefile.win _apached
```

Either command will compile Apache. The latter will disable optimization of the resulting files, making it easier to single step the code to find bugs and track down problems.

You can add your apr-util dbd and dbm provider choices with the additional make (environment) variables DBD_LIST and DBM_LIST, see the comments about [Optional] Database libraries, above. Review the initial comments in Makefile.win for additional options that can be provided when invoking the build.

50.3. Developer Studio Workspace IDE Build

Apache can also be compiled using VC++'s Visual Studio development environment. To simplify this process, a Visual Studio workspace, Apache.dsw, is provided. This workspace exposes the entire list of working .dsp projects that are required for the complete Apache binary release. It includes dependencies between the projects to assure that they are built in the appropriate order.

Open the Apache.dsw workspace, and select InstallBin (Release or Debug build, as desired) as the Active Project. InstallBin causes all related project to be built, and then invokes Makefile.win to move the compiled executables and dlls. You may personalize the INSTDIR= choice by changing InstallBin's Settings, General tab, Build command line entry. INSTDIR defaults to the /Apache2 directory. If you only want a test compile (without installing) you may build the BuildBin project instead.

The .dsp project files are distributed in Visual Studio 6.0 (98) format. Visual C++ 5.0 (97) will recognize them. Visual Studio 2002 (.NET) and later users must convert Apache.dsw plus the .dsp files into an Apache.sln plus .msproj files. Be sure you reconvert the .msproj file again if its source .dsp file changes! This is really trivial, just open Apache.dsw in the VC++ 7.0 IDE once again and reconvert.

There is a flaw in the .vcproj conversion of .dsp files. devenv.exe will mis-parse the /D flag for RC flags containing long quoted /D'efines which contain spaces. The command:

```
perl srclib\apr\build\cvtdsp.pl -2005
```

will convert the /D flags for RC flags to use an alternate, parseable syntax; unfortunately this syntax isn't supported by Visual Studio 97 or its exported .mak files. These /D flags are used to pass the long description of the mod_apachemodule.so files to the shared .rc resource version-identifier build.

Visual Studio 2002 (.NET) and later users should also use the Build menu, Configuration Manager dialog to uncheck both the Debug and Release Solution modules abs, mod_deflate and mod_ssl components, as well as every component starting with apr_db*. These modules are built by invoking nmake, or the IDE directly with the BinBuild target, which builds those modules conditionally if the srclib directories openssl and/or zlib exist, and based on the setting of DBD_LIST and DBM_LIST environment variables.

50.4. Exporting command-line .mak files

Exported .mak files pose a greater hassle, but they are required for Visual C++ 5.0 users to build mod_ssl, abs (*ab* with SSL support) and/or mod_deflate. The .mak files also support a broader range of C++ tool chain distributions, such as Visual Studio Express.

You must first build all projects in order to create all dynamic auto-generated targets, so that dependencies can be parsed correctly. Build the entire project from within the Visual Studio 6.0 (98) IDE, using the `BuildAll` target, then use the Project Menu Export for all makefiles (checking on "with dependencies".) Run the following command to correct absolute paths into relative paths so they will build anywhere:

```
perl srclib\apr\build\fixwin32mak.pl
```

You must type this command from the *top level* directory of the httpd source tree. Every `.mak` and `.dep` project file within the current directory and below will be corrected, and the timestamps adjusted to reflect the `.dsp`.

Always review the generated `.mak` and `.dep` files for Platform SDK or other local, machine specific file paths. The `DevStudio\Common\MSDev98\bin\` (VC6) directory contains a `sysincl.dat` file, which lists all exceptions. Update this file (including both forward and backslashed paths, such as both `sys/time.h` and `sys\time.h`) to ignore such newer dependencies. Including local-install paths in a distributed `.mak` file will cause the build to fail completely.

If you contribute back a patch that revises project files, we must commit project files in Visual Studio 6.0 format. Changes should be simple, with minimal compilation and linkage flags that can be recognized by all Visual Studio environments.

50.5. Installation

Once Apache has been compiled, it needs to be installed in its server root directory. The default is the `\Apache2` directory, of the same drive.

To build and install all the files into the desired folder *dir* automatically, use one of the following `nmake` commands:

```
nmake /f Makefile.win installr INSTDIR=dir
nmake /f Makefile.win installd INSTDIR=dir
```

The *dir* argument to `INSTDIR` provides the installation directory; it can be omitted if Apache is to be installed into `\Apache22` (of the current drive).

50.6. Warning about building Apache from the development tree

Note only the `.dsp` files are maintained between `release` builds. The `.mak` files are NOT regenerated, due to the tremendous waste of reviewer's time. Therefore, you cannot rely on the NMAKE commands above to build revised `.dsp` project files unless you then export all `.mak` files yourself from the project. This is unnecessary if you build from within the Microsoft Developer Studio environment.

Chapter 51.
Using Apache With Novell NetWare

This document explains how to install, configure and run Apache 2.0 under Novell NetWare 6.0 and above. If you find any bugs, or wish to contribute in other ways, please use our *bug reporting page*[1].

The bug reporting page and dev-httpd mailing list are *not* provided to answer questions about configuration or running Apache. Before you submit a bug report or request, first consult this document, the *Frequently Asked Questions* page and the other relevant documentation topics. If you still have a question or problem, post it to the *novell.devsup.webserver*[2] newsgroup, where many Apache users are more than willing to answer new and obscure questions about using Apache on NetWare.

Most of this document assumes that you are installing Apache from a binary distribution. If you want to compile Apache yourself (possibly to help with development, or to track down bugs), see the section on *Compiling Apache for NetWare* below.

51.1. Requirements

Apache 2.0 is designed to run on NetWare 6.0 service pack 3 and above. If you are running a service pack less than SP3, you must install the latest *NetWare Libraries for C (LibC)*[3].

NetWare service packs are available *here*[4].

Apache 2.0 for NetWare can also be run in a NetWare 5.1 environment as long as the latest service pack or the latest version of the *NetWare Libraries for C (LibC)*[5] has been installed . **WARNING:** Apache 2.0 for NetWare has not been targeted for or tested in this environment.

---

[1] *http://httpd.apache.org/bug_report.html*
[2] *news://developer-forums.novell.com/novell.devsup.webserver*
[3] *http://developer.novell.com/ndk/libc.htm*
[4] *http://support.novell.com/misc/patlst.htm#nw*
[5] *http://developer.novell.com/ndk/libc.htm*

51.2. Downloading Apache for NetWare

Information on the latest version of Apache can be found on the Apache web server at *http://www.apache.org/*. This will list the current release, any more recent alpha or beta-test releases, together with details of mirror web and anonymous ftp sites. Binary builds of the latest releases of Apache 2.0 for NetWare can be downloaded from *http://www.apache.org/dist/httpd/binaries/netware*.

51.3. Installing Apache for NetWare

There is no Apache install program for NetWare currently. If you are building Apache 2.0 for NetWare from source, you will need to copy the files over to the server manually.

Follow these steps to install Apache on NetWare from the binary download (assuming you will install to sys:/apache2):

- Unzip the binary download file to the root of the SYS: volume (may be installed to any volume)
- Edit the httpd.conf file setting <u>ServerRoot</u> and <u>ServerName</u> along with any file path values to reflect your correct server settings
- Add SYS:/APACHE2 to the search path, for example:

```
SEARCH ADD SYS:\APACHE2
```

Follow these steps to install Apache on NetWare manually from your own build source (assuming you will install to sys:/apache2):

- Create a directory called Apache2 on a NetWare volume
- Copy APACHE2.NLM, APRLIB.NLM to SYS:/APACHE2
- Create a directory under SYS:/APACHE2 called BIN
- Copy HTDIGEST.NLM, HTPASSWD.NLM, HTDBM.NLM, LOGRES.NLM, ROTLOGS.NLM to SYS:/APACHE2/BIN
- Create a directory under SYS:/APACHE2 called CONF
- Copy the HTTPD-STD.CONF file to the SYS:/APACHE2/CONF directory and rename to HTTPD.CONF
- Copy the MIME.TYPES, CHARSET.CONV and MAGIC files to SYS:/APACHE2/CONF directory
- Copy all files and subdirectories in \HTTPD-2.0\DOCS\ICONS to SYS:/APACHE2/ICONS
- Copy all files and subdirectories in \HTTPD-2.0\DOCS\MANUAL to SYS:/APACHE2/MANUAL

- Copy all files and subdirectories in \HTTPD-2.0\DOCS\ERROR to SYS:/APACHE2/ERROR

- Copy all files and subdirectories in \HTTPD-2.0\DOCS\DOCROOT to SYS:/APACHE2/HTDOCS

- Create the directory SYS:/APACHE2/LOGS on the server

- Create the directory SYS:/APACHE2/CGI-BIN on the server

- Create the directory SYS:/APACHE2/MODULES and copy all nlm modules into the modules directory

- Edit the HTTPD.CONF file searching for all @@Value@@ markers and replacing them with the appropriate setting

- Add SYS:/APACHE2 to the search path, for example:

```
SEARCH ADD SYS:\APACHE2
```

Apache may be installed to other volumes besides the default SYS volume.

During the build process, adding the keyword "install" to the makefile command line will automatically produce a complete distribution package under the subdirectory DIST. Install Apache by simply copying the distribution that was produced by the makfiles to the root of a NetWare volume (see: *Compiling Apache for NetWare* below).

51.4. Running Apache for NetWare

To start Apache just type apache at the console. This will load apache in the OS address space. If you prefer to load Apache in a protected address space you may specify the address space with the load statement as follows:

```
load address space = apache2 apache2
```

This will load Apache into an address space called apache2. Running multiple instances of Apache concurrently on NetWare is possible by loading each instance into its own protected address space.

After starting Apache, it will be listening to port 80 (unless you changed the Listen directive in the configuration files). To connect to the server and access the default page, launch a browser and enter the server's name or address. This should respond with a welcome page, and a link to the Apache manual. If nothing happens or you get an error, look in the error_log file in the logs directory.

Once your basic installation is working, you should configure it properly by editing the files in the conf directory.

To unload Apache running in the OS address space just type the following at the console:

```
unload apache2
```

or

```
apache2 shutdown
```

If apache is running in a protected address space specify the address space in the unload statement:

```
unload address space = apache2 apache2
```

When working with Apache it is important to know how it will find the configuration files. You can specify a configuration file on the command line in two ways:

-f specifies a path to a particular configuration file

```
apache2 -f "vol:/my server/conf/my.conf"
apache -f test/test.conf
```

In these cases, the proper ServerRoot should be set in the configuration file.

If you don't specify a configuration file name with -f, Apache will use the file name compiled into the server, usually conf/httpd.conf. Invoking Apache with the -V switch will display this value labeled as SERVER_CONFIG_FILE. Apache will then determine its ServerRoot by trying the following, in this order:

- A ServerRoot directive via a -C switch.
- The -d switch on the command line.
- Current working directory
- The server root compiled into the server.

The server root compiled into the server is usually sys:/apache2. invoking apache with the -V switch will display this value labeled as HTTPD_ROOT.

Apache 2.0 for NetWare includes a set of command line directives that can be used to modify or display information about the running instance of the web server. These directives are only available while Apache is running. Each of these directives must be preceded by the keyword APACHE2.

RESTART

Instructs Apache to terminate all running worker threads as they become idle, reread the configuration file and restart each worker thread based on the new configuration.

VERSION

Displays version information about the currently running instance of Apache.

MODULES

Displays a list of loaded modules both built-in and external.

DIRECTIVES

Displays a list of all available directives.

SETTINGS

Enables or disables the thread status display on the console. When enabled, the state of each running threads is displayed on the Apache console screen.

SHUTDOWN

Terminates the running instance of the Apache web server.

HELP

Describes each of the runtime directives.

By default these directives are issued against the instance of Apache running in the OS address space. To issue a directive against a specific instance running in a protected address space, include the -p parameter along with the name of the address space. For more information type "apache2 Help" on the command line.

51.5. Configuring Apache for NetWare

Apache is configured by reading configuration files usually stored in the conf directory. These are the same as files used to configure the Unix version, but there are a few different directives for Apache on NetWare. See the *Apache documentation* for all the available directives.

The main differences in Apache for NetWare are:

- Because Apache for NetWare is multithreaded, it does not use a separate process for each request, as Apache does on some Unix implementations. Instead there are only threads running: a parent thread, and multiple child or worker threads which handle the requests.

  Therefore the "process"-management directives are different:

  MaxRequestsPerChild - Like the Unix directive, this controls how many requests a worker thread will serve before exiting. The recommended default, MaxRequestsPerChild 0, causes the thread to continue servicing request indefinitely. It is recommended on NetWare, unless there is some specific reason, that this directive always remain set to 0.

  StartThreads - This directive tells the server how many threads it should start initially. The recommended default is StartThreads 50.

MinSpareThreads - This directive instructs the server to spawn additional worker threads if the number of idle threads ever falls below this value. The recommended default is MinSpareThreads 10.

MaxSpareThreads - This directive instructs the server to begin terminating worker threads if the number of idle threads ever exceeds this value. The recommended default is MaxSpareThreads 100.

MaxThreads - This directive limits the total number of work threads to a maximum value. The recommended default is ThreadsPerChild 250.

ThreadStackSize - This directive tells the server what size of stack to use for the individual worker thread. The recommended default is ThreadStackSize 65536.

- The directives that accept filenames as arguments must use NetWare filenames instead of Unix names. However, because Apache uses Unix-style names internally, forward slashes must be used rather than backslashes. It is recommended that all rooted file paths begin with a volume name. If omitted, Apache will assume the SYS: volume which may not be correct.

- Apache for NetWare has the ability to load modules at runtime, without recompiling the server. If Apache is compiled normally, it will install a number of optional modules in the \Apache2\modules directory. To activate these, or other modules, the LoadModule directive must be used. For example, to active the status module, use the following:

```
LoadModule status_module modules/status.nlm
```

Information on *creating loadable modules* is also available.

Additional NetWare specific directives:

- CGIMapExtension - This directive maps a CGI file extension to a script interpreter.
- SecureListen - Enables SSL encryption for a specified port.
- NWSSLTrustedCerts - Adds trusted certificates that are used to create secure connections to proxied servers.
- NWSSLUpgradeable - Allow a connection created on the specified address/port to be upgraded to an SSL connection.

51.6. Compiling Apache for NetWare

Compiling Apache requires MetroWerks CodeWarrior 6.x or higher. Once Apache has been built, it can be installed to the root of any NetWare volume. The default is the sys:/Apache2 directory.

Before running the server you must fill out the conf directory. Copy the file HTTPD-STD.CONF from the distribution conf directory and rename it to HTTPD.CONF. Edit the HTTPD.CONF file searching for all @@Value@@ markers and replacing them with the appropriate setting. Copy over the conf/magic and conf/mime.types files as well. Alternatively, a complete distribution can be built by including the keyword install when invoking the makefiles.

Requirements:

The following development tools are required to build Apache 2.0 for NetWare:

- Metrowerks CodeWarrior 6.0 or higher with the *NetWare PDK 3.0*[6] or higher.
- *NetWare Libraries for C (LibC)*[7]
- *LDAP Libraries for C*[8]
- *ZLIB Compression Library source code*[9]
- AWK utility (awk, gawk or similar). AWK can be downloaded from *http://developer.novell.com/ndk/apache.htm*. The utility must be found in your windows path and must be named awk.exe.
- To build using the makefiles, you will need GNU make version 3.78.1 (GMake) available at *http://developer.novell.com/ndk/apache.htm*.

Building Apache using the NetWare makefiles:

- Set the environment variable NOVELLLIBC to the location of the NetWare Libraries for C SDK, for example:

```
Set NOVELLLIBC=c:\novell\ndk\libc
```

- Set the environment variable METROWERKS to the location where you installed the Metrowerks CodeWarrior compiler, for example:

```
Set METROWERKS=C:\Program Files\Metrowerks\CodeWarrior
```

  If you installed to the default location C:\Program Files\Metrowerks\CodeWarrior, you don't need to set this.

- Set the environment variable LDAPSDK to the location where you installed the LDAP Libraries for C, for example:

---

[6] *http://developer.novell.com/ndk/cwpdk.htm*
[7] *http://developer.novell.com/ndk/libc.htm*
[8] *http://developer.novell.com/ndk/cldap.htm*
[9] *http://www.gzip.org/zlib/*

```
Set LDAPSDK=c:\Novell\NDK\cldapsdk\NetWare\libc
```

- Set the environment variable ZLIBSDK to the location where you installed the source code for the ZLib Library, for example:

```
Set ZLIBSDK=D:\NOVELL\zlib
```

- Set the environment variable AP_WORK to the full path of the httpd source code directory.

```
Set AP_WORK=D:\httpd-2.0.x
```

- Set the environment variable APR_WORK to the full path of the apr source code directory. Typically \httpd\srclib\apr but the APR project can be outside of the httpd directory structure.

```
Set APR_WORK=D:\apr-1.x.x
```

- Set the environment variable APU_WORK to the full path of the apr-util source code directory. Typically \httpd\srclib\apr-util but the APR-UTIL project can be outside of the httpd directory structure.

```
Set APU_WORK=D:\apr-util-1.x.x
```

- Make sure that the path to the AWK utility and the GNU make utility (gmake.exe) have been included in the system's PATH environment variable.
- Download the source code and unzip to an appropriate directory on your workstation.
- Change directory to \httpd-2.0 and build the prebuild utilities by running "gmake -f nwgnumakefile prebuild". This target will create the directory \httpd-2.0\nwprebuild and copy each of the utilities to this location that are necessary to complete the following build steps.
- Copy the files \httpd-2.0\nwprebuild\GENCHARS.nlm and \httpd-2.0\nwprebuild\DFTABLES.nlm to the SYS: volume of a NetWare server and run them using the following commands:

```
SYS:\genchars > sys:\test_char.h
SYS:\dftables sys:\chartables.c
```

- Copy the files test_char.h and chartables.c to the directory \httpd-2.0\os\netware on the build machine.
- Change directory to \httpd-2.0 and build Apache by running "gmake -f nwgnumakefile". You can create a distribution directory by adding an install parameter to the command, for example:

```
gmake -f nwgnumakefile install
```

51.6.1. Additional make options

- `gmake -f nwgnumakefile`

  Builds release versions of all of the binaries and copies them to a `\release` destination directory.

- `gmake -f nwgnumakefile DEBUG=1`

  Builds debug versions of all of the binaries and copies them to a `\debug` destination directory.

- `gmake -f nwgnumakefile install`

  Creates a complete Apache distribution with binaries, docs and additional support files in a `\dist\Apache2` directory.

- `gmake -f nwgnumakefile prebuild`

  Builds all of the prebuild utilities and copies them to the `\nwprebuild` directory.

- `gmake -f nwgnumakefile installdev`

  Same as install but also creates a `\lib` and `\include` directory in the destination directory and copies headers and import files.

- `gmake -f nwgnumakefile clean`

  Cleans all object files and binaries from the `\release.o` or `\debug.o` build areas depending on whether DEBUG has been defined.

- `gmake -f nwgnumakefile clobber_all`

  Same as clean and also deletes the distribution directory if it exists.

51.6.2. Additional environment variable options

- To build all of the experimental modules, set the environment variable EXPERIMENTAL:

  ```
  Set EXPERIMENTAL=1
  ```

- To build Apache using standard BSD style sockets rather than Winsock, set the environment variable USE_STDSOCKETS:

  ```
  Set USE_STDSOCKETS=1
  ```

Building mod_ssl for the NetWare platform

By default Apache for NetWare uses the built-in module mod_nw_ssl to provide SSL services. This module simply enables the native SSL services implemented in NetWare OS to handle all encryption for a given port. Alternatively, mod_ssl can also be used in the same manner as on other platforms.

Before mod_ssl can be built for the NetWare platform, the OpenSSL libraries must be provided. This can be done through the following steps:

- Download the recent OpenSSL 0.9.8 release source code from the *OpenSSL Source*[10] page (older 0.9.7 versions need to be patched and are therefore not recommended).
- Edit the file `NetWare/set_env.bat` and modify any tools and utilities paths so that they correspond to your build environment.
- From the root of the OpenSSL source directory, run the following scripts:

```
Netware\set_env netware-libc
Netware\build netware-libc
```

  For performance reasons you should enable to build with ASM code. Download NASM from the *SF site*[11]. Then configure OpenSSL to use ASM code:

```
Netware\build netware-libc nw-nasm enable-mdc2 enable-md5
```

  Warning: dont use the CodeWarrior Assembler - it produces broken code!

- Before building Apache, set the environment variable `OSSLSDK` to the full path to the root of the openssl source code directory, and set WITH_MOD_SSL to 1.

```
Set OSSLSDK=d:\openssl-0.9.8x
Set WITH_MOD_SSL=1
```

---

[10] *http://www.openssl.org/source/*
[11] *http://nasm.sourceforge.net/*

Chapter 52.

Running a High-Performance Web Server on HPUX

```
Date: Wed, 05 Nov 1997 16:59:34 -0800
From: Rick Jones <raj@cup.hp.com>
Reply-To: raj@cup.hp.com
Organization: Network Performance
Subject: HP-UX tuning tips
```

Here are some tuning tips for HP-UX to add to the tuning page.

For HP-UX 9.X: Upgrade to 10.20
For HP-UX 10.[00|01|10]: Upgrade to 10.20

For HP-UX 10.20:

Install the latest cumulative ARPA Transport Patch. This will allow you to configure the size of the TCP connection lookup hash table. The default is 256 buckets and must be set to a power of two. This is accomplished with adb against the *disc* image of the kernel. The variable name is tcp_hash_size. Notice that it's critically important that you use "W" to write a 32 bit quantity, not "w" to write a 16 bit value when patching the disc image because the tcp_hash_size variable is a 32 bit quantity.

How to pick the value? Examine the output of *ftp://ftp.cup.hp.com/dist/networking/tools/connhist* and see how many total TCP connections exist on the system. You probably want that number divided by the hash table size to be reasonably small, say less than 10. Folks can look at HP's SPECweb96 disclosures for some common settings. These can be found at *http://www.specbench.org/*. If an HP-UX system was performing at 1000 SPECweb96 connections per second, the TIME_WAIT time of 60 seconds would mean 60,000 TCP "connections" being tracked.

Folks can check their listen queue depths with *ftp://ftp.cup.hp.com/dist/networking/misc/listenq*.

If folks are running Apache on a PA-8000 based system, they should consider "chatr'ing" the Apache executable to have a large page size. This would be "chatr +pi L <BINARY>". The GID of the running executable must have MLOCK privileges. Setprivgrp(1m) should be consulted for assigning MLOCK. The change can be validated by running Glance and examining the memory regions of the server(s) to make sure that they show a non-trivial fraction of the text segment being locked.

If folks are running Apache on MP systems, they might consider writing a small program that uses mpctl() to bind processes to processors. A simple pid % numcpu algorithm is probably sufficient. This might even go into the source code.

If folks are concerned about the number of FIN_WAIT_2 connections, they can use nettune to shrink the value of tcp_keepstart. However, they should be careful there - certainly do not make it less than oh two to four minutes. If tcp_hash_size has been set well, it is probably OK to let the FIN_WAIT_2's take longer to timeout (perhaps even the default two hours) - they will not on average have a big impact on performance.

There are other things that could go into the code base, but that might be left for another email. Feel free to drop me a message if you or others are interested.

sincerely,

rick jones

http://www.netperf.org/netperf/

Chapter 53.
The Apache EBCDIC Port

> **Warning:** This document has not been updated to take into account changes made in the 2.0 version of the Apache HTTP Server. Some of the information may still be relevant, but please use it with care.

53.1. Overview of the Apache EBCDIC Port

Version 1.3 of the Apache HTTP Server is the first version which includes a port to a (non-ASCII) mainframe machine which uses the EBCDIC character set as its native codeset.

(It is the SIEMENS family of mainframes running the *BS2000/OSD operating system*[1]. This mainframe OS nowadays features a SVR4-derived POSIX subsystem).

The port was started initially to

- prove the feasibility of porting *the Apache HTTP server*[2] to this platform
- find a "worthy and capable" successor for the venerable *CERN-3.0*[3] daemon (which was ported a couple of years ago), and to
- prove that Apache's preforking process model can on this platform easily outperform the accept-fork-serve model used by CERN by a factor of 5 or more.

This document serves as a rationale to describe some of the design decisions of the port to this machine.

53.2. Design Goals

One objective of the EBCDIC port was to maintain enough backwards compatibility with the (EBCDIC) CERN server to make the transition to the new server attractive and easy. This required the addition of a configurable method to define whether a HTML document was stored in ASCII (the only format accepted by the old server) or in EBCDIC (the native

---

[1] *http://www.siemens.de/servers/bs2osd/osdbc_us.htm*
[2] *http://httpd.apache.org/*
[3] *http://www.w3.org/Daemon/*

document format in the POSIX subsystem, and therefore the only realistic format in which the other POSIX tools like grep or sed could operate on the documents). The current solution to this is a "pseudo-MIME-format" which is intercepted and interpreted by the Apache server (see below). Future versions might solve the problem by defining an "ebcdic-handler" for all documents which must be converted.

53.3. Technical Solution

Since all Apache input and output is based upon the BUFF data type and its methods, the easiest solution was to add the conversion to the BUFF handling routines. The conversion must be settable at any time, so a BUFF flag was added which defines whether a BUFF object has currently enabled conversion or not. This flag is modified at several points in the HTTP protocol:

- **set** before a request is received (because the request and the request header lines are always in ASCII format)
- **set/unset** when the request body is received - depending on the content type of the request body (because the request body may contain ASCII text or a binary file)
- **set** before a reply header is sent (because the response header lines are always in ASCII format)
- **set/unset** when the response body is sent - depending on the content type of the response body (because the response body may contain text or a binary file)

53.4. Porting Notes

1. The relevant changes in the source are #ifdef'ed into two categories:

    #ifdef CHARSET_EBCDIC

    Code which is needed for any EBCDIC based machine. This includes character translations, differences in contiguity of the two character sets, flags which indicate which part of the HTTP protocol has to be converted and which part doesn't *etc.*

    #ifdef _OSD_POSIX

    Code which is needed for the SIEMENS BS2000/OSD mainframe platform only. This deals with include file differences and socket implementation topics which are only required on the BS2000/OSD platform.

2. The possibility to translate between ASCII and EBCDIC at the socket level (on BS2000 POSIX, there is a socket option which supports this) was intentionally *not* chosen, because the byte stream at the HTTP protocol level consists of a mixture of protocol related strings and non-protocol related raw file data. HTTP protocol

strings are always encoded in ASCII (the GET request, any Header: lines, the chunking information *etc.*) whereas the file transfer parts (*i.e.*, GIF images, CGI output *etc.*) should usually be just "passed through" by the server. This separation between "protocol string" and "raw data" is reflected in the server code by functions like bgets() or rvputs() for strings, and functions like bwrite() for binary data. A global translation of everything would therefore be inadequate.

(In the case of text files of course, provisions must be made so that EBCDIC documents are always served in ASCII)

3. This port therefore features a built-in protocol level conversion for the server-internal strings (which the compiler translated to EBCDIC strings) and thus for all server-generated documents. The hard coded ASCII escapes \012 and \015 which are ubiquitous in the server code are an exception: they are already the binary encoding of the ASCII \n and \r and must not be converted to ASCII a second time. This exception is only relevant for server-generated strings; and *external* EBCDIC documents are not expected to contain ASCII newline characters.

4. By examining the call hierarchy for the BUFF management routines, I added an "ebcdic/ascii conversion layer" which would be crossed on every puts/write/get/gets, and a conversion flag which allowed enabling/disabling the conversions on-the-fly. Usually, a document crosses this layer twice from its origin source (a file or CGI output) to its destination (the requesting client): file -> Apache, and Apache -> client.

The server can now read the header lines of a CGI-script output in EBCDIC format, and then find out that the remainder of the script's output is in ASCII (like in the case of the output of a WWW Counter program: the document body contains a GIF image). All header processing is done in the native EBCDIC format; the server then determines, based on the type of document being served, whether the document body (except for the chunking information, of course) is in ASCII already or must be converted from EBCDIC.

5. For Text documents (MIME types text/plain, text/html *etc.*), an implicit translation to ASCII can be used, or (if the users prefer to store some documents in raw ASCII form for faster serving, or because the files reside on a NFS-mounted directory tree) can be served without conversion.

Example:

to serve files with the suffix .ahtml as a raw ASCII text/html document without implicit conversion (and suffix .ascii as ASCII text/plain), use the directives:

```
AddType text/x-ascii-html .ahtml
AddType text/x-ascii-plain .ascii
```

Similarly, any `text/foo` MIME type can be served as "raw ASCII" by configuring a MIME type `"text/x-ascii-foo"` for it using `AddType`.

6. Non-text documents are always served "binary" without conversion. This seems to be the most sensible choice for, *.e.g.,* GIF/ZIP/AU file types. This of course requires the user to copy them to the mainframe host using the `"rcp -b"` binary switch.

7. Server parsed files are always assumed to be in native (*i.e.,* EBCDIC) format as used on the machine, and are converted after processing.

8. For CGI output, the CGI script determines whether a conversion is needed or not: by setting the appropriate Content-Type, text files can be converted, or GIF output can be passed through unmodified. An example for the latter case is the wwwcount program which we ported as well.

53.5. Document Storage Notes

Binary Files

All files with a `Content-Type:` which does not start with `text/` are regarded as *binary files* by the server and are not subject to any conversion. Examples for binary files are GIF images, gzip-compressed files and the like.

When exchanging binary files between the mainframe host and a Unix machine or Windows PC, be sure to use the ftp "binary" (`TYPE I`) command, or use the `rcp -b` command from the mainframe host (the `-b` switch is not supported in unix `rcp`'s).

Text Documents

The default assumption of the server is that Text Files (*i.e.,* all files whose `Content-Type:` starts with `text/`) are stored in the native character set of the host, EBCDIC.

Server Side Included Documents

SSI documents must currently be stored in EBCDIC only. No provision is made to convert it from ASCII before processing.

53.6. Apache Modules' Status

Module	Status	Notes
core	+	
mod_access	+	
mod_actions	+	
mod_alias	+	

Module	Status	Notes
mod_asis	+	
mod_auth	+	
mod_auth_anon	+	
mod_auth_dbm	?	with own libdb.a
mod_autoindex	+	
mod_cern_meta	?	
mod_cgi	+	
mod_digest	+	
mod_dir	+	
mod_so	-	no shared libs
mod_env	+	
mod_example	-	(test bed only)
mod_expires	+	
mod_headers	+	
mod_imagemap	+	
mod_include	+	
mod_info	+	
mod_log_agent	+	
mod_log_config	+	
mod_log_referer	+	
mod_mime	+	
mod_mime_magic	?	not ported yet
mod_negotiation	+	
mod_proxy	+	
mod_rewrite	+	untested
mod_setenvif	+	
mod_speling	+	
mod_status	+	
mod_unique_id	+	
mod_userdir	+	
mod_usertrack	?	untested

53.7. Third Party Modules' Status

Module	Status	Notes
mod_jserv[4]	-	JAVA still being ported.
mod_php3[5]	+	mod_php3 runs fine, with LDAP and GD and FreeType libraries.
mod_put[6]	?	untested
mod_session[7]	-	untested

---

[4] *http://java.apache.org/*

[5] *http://www.php.net/*

[6] *http://hpwww.ec-lyon.fr/~vincent/apache/mod_put.html*

[7] *ftp://hachiman.vidya.com/pub/apache/*

Part VIII.

Server and Supporting Programs

This page documents all the executable programs included with the Apache HTTP Server.

Index

httpd

Apache hypertext transfer protocol server

apachectl

Apache HTTP server control interface

ab

Apache HTTP server benchmarking tool

apxs

APache eXtenSion tool

configure

Configure the source tree

dbmmanage

Create and update user authentication files in DBM format for basic authentication

htcacheclean

Clean up the disk cache

htdigest

Create and update user authentication files for digest authentication

htdbm

Manipulate DBM password databases.

htpasswd

Create and update user authentication files for basic authentication

httxt2dbm

Create dbm files for use with RewriteMap

logresolve

Resolve hostnames for IP-addresses in Apache logfiles

rotatelogs

Rotate Apache logs without having to kill the server

suexec

Switch User For Exec

Other Programs

Support tools with no own manual page.

Chapter 54.

httpd - Apache Hypertext Transfer Protocol Server

`httpd` is the Apache HyperText Transfer Protocol (HTTP) server program. It is designed to be run as a standalone daemon process. When used like this it will create a pool of child processes or threads to handle requests.

In general, `httpd` should not be invoked directly, but rather should be invoked via `apachectl` on Unix-based systems or *as a service on Windows NT, 2000 and XP* and *as a console application on Windows 9x and ME.*

Synopsis

`httpd` [`-d` *serverroot*] [`-f` *config*] [`-C` *directive*] [`-c` *directive*] [`-D` *parameter*] [`-e` *level*] [`-E` *file*] [`-k` start|restart|graceful|stop|graceful-stop] [`-R` *directory*] [`-h`] [`-l`] [`-L`] [`-S`] [`-t`] [`-v`] [`-V`] [`-X`] [`-M`]

On *Windows systems*, the following additional arguments are available:

`httpd` [`-k` install|config|uninstall] [`-n` *name*] [`-w`]

Options

-d *serverroot*

Set the initial value for the <u>ServerRoot</u> directive to *serverroot*. This can be overridden by the ServerRoot directive in the configuration file. The default is `/usr/local/apache2`.

-f *config*

Uses the directives in the file *config* on startup. If *config* does not begin with a /, then it is taken to be a path relative to the <u>ServerRoot</u>. The default is `conf/httpd.conf`.

-k `start|restart|graceful|stop|graceful-stop`

Signals `httpd` to start, restart, or stop. See *Stopping Apache* for more information.

-C *directive*

Process the configuration *directive* before reading config files.

-c *directive*

Process the configuration *directive* after reading config files.

-D *parameter*

Sets a configuration *parameter* which can be used with `<IfDefine>` sections in the configuration files to conditionally skip or process commands at server startup and restart. Also can be used to set certain less-common startup parameters including -DNO_DETACH (prevent the parent from forking) and -DFOREGROUND (prevent the parent from calling `setsid()` et al).

-e *level*

Sets the `LogLevel` to *level* during server startup. This is useful for temporarily increasing the verbosity of the error messages to find problems during startup.

-E *file*

Send error messages during server startup to *file*.

-R *directory*

When the server is compiled using the SHARED_CORE rule, this specifies the *directory* for the shared object files.

-h

Output a short summary of available command line options.

-l

Output a list of modules compiled into the server. This will **not** list dynamically loaded modules included using the `LoadModule` directive.

-L

Output a list of directives together with expected arguments and places where the directive is valid.

-M

Dump a list of loaded Static and Shared Modules.

-S

Show the settings as parsed from the config file (currently only shows the virtualhost settings).

-t

> Run syntax tests for configuration files only. The program immediately exits after these syntax parsing tests with either a return code of 0 (Syntax OK) or return code not equal to 0 (Syntax Error). If -D *DUMP_VHOSTS* is also set, details of the virtual host configuration will be printed. If -D *DUMP_MODULES* is set, all loaded modules will be printed.

-v

> Print the version of `httpd`, and then exit.

-V

> Print the version and build parameters of `httpd`, and then exit.

-X

> Run httpd in debug mode. Only one worker will be started and the server will not detach from the console.

The following arguments are available only on the *Windows platform*:

-k install|config|uninstall

> Install Apache as a Windows NT service; change startup options for the Apache service; and uninstall the Apache service.

-n *name*

> The *name* of the Apache service to signal.

-w

> Keep the console window open on error so that the error message can be read.

Chapter 55.
ab - Apache HTTP server benchmarking tool

ab is a tool for benchmarking your Apache Hypertext Transfer Protocol (HTTP) server. It is designed to give you an impression of how your current Apache installation performs. This especially shows you how many requests per second your Apache installation is capable of serving.

Synopsis

ab [-A *auth-username*:*password*] [-b *windowsize*] [-c *concurrency*] [-C *cookie-name=value*] [-d] [-e *csv-file*] [-f *protocol*] [-g *gnuplot-file*] [-h] [-H *custom-header*] [-i] [-k] [-n *requests*] [-p *POST-file*] [-P *proxy-auth-username*:*password*] [-q] [-r] [-s] [-S] [-t *timelimit*] [-T *content-type*] [-u *PUT-file*] [-v *verbosity*] [-V] [-w] [-x *<table>-attributes*] [-X *proxy*[:*port*]] [-y *<tr>-attributes*] [-z *<td>-attributes*] [-Z *ciphersuite*] [http[s]://]*hostname*[:*port*]/*path*

Options

-A *auth-username*:*password*

    Supply BASIC Authentication credentials to the server. The username and password are separated by a single : and sent on the wire base64 encoded. The string is sent regardless of whether the server needs it (*i.e.,* has sent an 401 authentication needed).

-b *windowsize*

    Size of TCP send/receive buffer, in bytes.

-c *concurrency*

    Number of multiple requests to perform at a time. Default is one request at a time.

-C *cookie-name=value*

    Add a Cookie: line to the request. The argument is typically in the form of a *name=value* pair. This field is repeatable.

-d

Do not display the "percentage served within XX [ms] table". (legacy support).

-e *csv-file*

Write a Comma separated value (CSV) file which contains for each percentage (from 1% to 100%) the time (in milliseconds) it took to serve that percentage of the requests. This is usually more useful than the 'gnuplot' file; as the results are already 'binned'.

-f *protocol*

Specify SSL/TLS protocol (SSL2, SSL3, TLS1, or ALL).

-g *gnuplot-file*

Write all measured values out as a 'gnuplot' or TSV (Tab separate values) file. This file can easily be imported into packages like Gnuplot, IDL, Mathematica, Igor or even Excel. The labels are on the first line of the file.

-h

Display usage information.

-H *custom-header*

Append extra headers to the request. The argument is typically in the form of a valid header line, containing a colon-separated field-value pair (*i.e.*, `"Accept-Encoding: zip/zop;8bit"`).

-i

Do `HEAD` requests instead of `GET`.

-k

Enable the HTTP KeepAlive feature, *i.e.,* perform multiple requests within one HTTP session. Default is no KeepAlive.

-n *requests*

Number of requests to perform for the benchmarking session. The default is to just perform a single request which usually leads to non-representative benchmarking results.

-p *POST-file*

File containing data to POST. Remember to also set `-T`.

-P *proxy-auth-username:password*

Supply BASIC Authentication credentials to a proxy en-route. The username and password are separated by a single : and sent on the wire base64 encoded. The string is sent regardless of whether the proxy needs it (*i.e.*, has sent an 407 proxy authentication needed).

-q

When processing more than 150 requests, ab outputs a progress count on stderr every 10% or 100 requests or so. The -q flag will suppress these messages.

-r

Don't exit on socket receive errors.

-s

When compiled in (ab -h will show you) use the SSL protected https rather than the http protocol. This feature is experimental and *very* rudimentary. You probably do not want to use it.

-S

Do not display the median and standard deviation values, nor display the warning/error messages when the average and median are more than one or two times the standard deviation apart. And default to the min/avg/max values. (legacy support).

-t *timelimit*

Maximum number of seconds to spend for benchmarking. This implies a -n 50000 internally. Use this to benchmark the server within a fixed total amount of time. Per default there is no timelimit.

-T *content-type*

Content-type header to use for POST/PUT data, eg. application/x-www-form-urlencoded. Default: text/plain.

-u *PUT-file*

File containing data to PUT. Remember to also set -T.

-v *verbosity*

Set verbosity level - 4 and above prints information on headers, 3 and above prints response codes (404, 200, etc.), 2 and above prints warnings and info.

-V

Display version number and exit.

-w

Print out results in HTML tables. Default table is two columns wide, with a white background.

-x *<table>-attributes*

String to use as attributes for `<table>`. Attributes are inserted `<table` *here* `>`.

-X *proxy* `[:port]`

Use a proxy server for the requests.

-y *<tr>-attributes*

String to use as attributes for `<tr>`.

-z *<td>-attributes*

String to use as attributes for `<td>`.

-Z *ciphersuite*

Specify SSL/TLS cipher suite (See openssl ciphers).

Bugs

There are various statically declared buffers of fixed length. Combined with the lazy parsing of the command line arguments, the response headers from the server and other external inputs, this might bite you.

It does not implement HTTP/1.x fully; only accepts some 'expected' forms of responses. The rather heavy use of `strstr(3)` shows up top in profile, which might indicate a performance problem; *i.e.*, you would measure the ab performance rather than the server's.

Chapter 56.
apachectl - Apache HTTP Server Control Interface

apachectl is a front end to the Apache HyperText Transfer Protocol (HTTP) server. It is designed to help the administrator control the functioning of the Apache *httpd* daemon.

The apachectl script can operate in two modes. First, it can act as a simple front-end to the *httpd* command that simply sets any necessary environment variables and then invokes *httpd*, passing through any command line arguments. Second, apachectl can act as a SysV init script, taking simple one-word arguments like start, restart, and stop, and translating them into appropriate signals to *httpd*.

If your Apache installation uses non-standard paths, you will need to edit the apachectl script to set the appropriate paths to the *httpd* binary. You can also specify any necessary *httpd* command line arguments. See the comments in the script for details.

The apachectl script returns a 0 exit value on success, and >0 if an error occurs. For more details, view the comments in the script.

Synopsis

When acting in pass-through mode, apachectl can take all the arguments available for the *httpd* binary.

apachectl [*httpd-argument*]

When acting in SysV init mode, apachectl takes simple, one-word commands, defined below.

apachectl *command*

Options

Only the SysV init-style options are defined here. Other arguments are defined on the *httpd* manual page.

start

> Start the Apache *httpd* daemon. Gives an error if it is already running. This is equivalent to `apachectl -k start`.

stop

> Stops the Apache *httpd* daemon. This is equivalent to `apachectl -k stop`.

restart

> Restarts the Apache *httpd* daemon. If the daemon is not running, it is started. This command automatically checks the configuration files as in `configtest` before initiating the restart to make sure the daemon doesn't die. This is equivalent to `apachectl -k restart`.

Fullstatus

> Displays a full status report from <u>mod_status</u>. For this to work, you need to have <u>mod_status</u> enabled on your server and a text-based browser such as `lynx` available on your system. The URL used to access the status report can be set by editing the `STATUSURL` variable in the script.

status

> Displays a brief status report. Similar to the `fullstatus` option, except that the list of requests currently being served is omitted.

graceful

> Gracefully restarts the Apache *httpd* daemon. If the daemon is not running, it is started. This differs from a normal restart in that currently open connections are not aborted. A side effect is that old log files will not be closed immediately. This means that if used in a log rotation script, a substantial delay may be necessary to ensure that the old log files are closed before processing them. This command automatically checks the configuration files as in `configtest` before initiating the restart to make sure Apache doesn't die. This is equivalent to `apachectl -k graceful`.

graceful-stop

> Gracefully stops the Apache *httpd* daemon. This differs from a normal stop in that currently open connections are not aborted. A side effect is that old log files will not be closed immediately. This is equivalent to `apachectl -k graceful-stop`.

configtest

> Run a configuration file syntax test. It parses the configuration files and either reports `Syntax Ok` or detailed information about the particular syntax error. This is equivalent to `apachectl -t`.

The following option was available in earlier versions but has been removed.

startssl

To start *httpd* with SSL support, you should edit your configuration file to include the relevant directives and then use the normal `apachectl start`.

Chapter 57.
apxs - APache eXtenSion tool

apxs is a tool for building and installing extension modules for the Apache HyperText Transfer Protocol (HTTP) server. This is achieved by building a dynamic shared object (DSO) from one or more source or object *files* which then can be loaded into the Apache server under runtime via the LoadModule directive from mod_so.

So to use this extension mechanism your platform has to support the DSO feature and your Apache *httpd* binary has to be built with the mod_so module. The apxs tool automatically complains if this is not the case. You can check this yourself by manually running the command

```
$ httpd -l
```

The module mod_so should be part of the displayed list. If these requirements are fulfilled you can easily extend your Apache server's functionality by installing your own modules with the DSO mechanism by the help of this apxs tool:

```
$ apxs -i -a -c mod_foo.c
gcc -fpic -DSHARED_MODULE -I/path/to/apache/include -c mod_foo.c
ld -Bshareable -o mod_foo.so mod_foo.o
cp mod_foo.so /path/to/apache/modules/mod_foo.so
chmod 755 /path/to/apache/modules/mod_foo.so
[activating module `foo' in /path/to/apache/etc/httpd.conf]
$ apachectl restart
/path/to/apache/sbin/apachectl restart: httpd not running, trying to start
[Tue Mar 31 11:27:55 1998] [debug] mod_so.c(303): loaded module foo_module
/path/to/apache/sbin/apachectl restart: httpd started
$ _
```

The arguments *files* can be any C source file (.c), a object file (.o) or even a library archive (.a). The apxs tool automatically recognizes these extensions and automatically used the C source files for compilation while just using the object and archive files for the linking phase. But when using such pre-compiled objects make sure they are compiled for position independent code (PIC) to be able to use them for a dynamically loaded shared object. For instance with GCC you always just have to use -fpic. For other C compilers consult its manual page or at watch for the flags apxs uses to compile the object files.

For more details about DSO support in Apache read the documentation of <u>mod_so</u> or perhaps even read the `src/modules/standard/mod_so.c` source file.

Synopsis

`apxs` -g [-S *name=value*] -n *modname*

`apxs` -q [-S *name=value*] *query* . . .

`apxs` -c [-S *name=value*] [-o *dsofile*] [-I *incdir*] [-D *name=value*]
[-L *libdir*] [-l *libname*] [-Wc,*compiler-flags*] [-Wl,*linker-flags*] *files* . . .

`apxs` -i [-S *name=value*] [-n *modname*] [-a] [-A] *dso-file* . . .

`apxs` -e [-S *name=value*] [-n *modname*] [-a] [-A] *dso-file* . . .

Options

Common Options

-n *modname*

> This explicitly sets the module name for the -i (install) and -g (template generation) option. Use this to explicitly specify the module name. For option -g this is required, for option -i the `apxs` tool tries to determine the name from the source or (as a fallback) at least by guessing it from the filename.

Query Options

-q

> Performs a query for `apxs`'s knowledge about certain settings. The *query* parameters can be one or more of the following strings: CC, CFLAGS, CFLAGS_SHLIB, INCLUDEDIR, LD_SHLIB, LDFLAGS_SHLIB, LIBEXECDIR, LIBS_SHLIB, SBINDIR, SYSCONFDIR, TARGET.
>
> Use this for manually determining settings. For instance use

```
INC=-I`apxs -q INCLUDEDIR`
```

> inside your own Makefiles if you need manual access to Apache's C header files.

Configuration Options

-S *name=value*

> This option changes the apxs settings described above.

Template Generation Options

-g

This generates a subdirectory *name* (see option -n) and there two files: A sample module source file named mod_*name*.c which can be used as a template for creating your own modules or as a quick start for playing with the apxs mechanism. And a corresponding Makefile for even easier build and installing of this module.

DSO Compilation Options

-c

This indicates the compilation operation. It first compiles the C source files (.c) of *files* into corresponding object files (.o) and then builds a dynamically shared object in *dsofile* by linking these object files plus the remaining object files (.o and .a) of *files*. If no -o option is specified the output file is guessed from the first filename in *files* and thus usually defaults to mod_*name*.so.

-o *dsofile*

Explicitly specifies the filename of the created dynamically shared object. If not specified and the name cannot be guessed from the *files* list, the fallback name mod_unknown.so is used.

-D *name=value*

This option is directly passed through to the compilation command(s). Use this to add your own defines to the build process.

-I *incdir*

This option is directly passed through to the compilation command(s). Use this to add your own include directories to search to the build process.

-L *libdir*

This option is directly passed through to the linker command. Use this to add your own library directories to search to the build process.

-l *libname*

This option is directly passed through to the linker command. Use this to add your own libraries to search to the build process.

-Wc, *compiler-flags*

This option passes *compiler-flags* as additional flags to the libtool --mode=compile command. Use this to add local compiler-specific options.

-Wl, *linker-flags*

> This option passes *linker-flags* as additional flags to the `libtool --mode=link` command. Use this to add local linker-specific options.

DSO Installation and Configuration Options

-i

> This indicates the installation operation and installs one or more dynamically shared objects into the server's *modules* directory.

-a

> This activates the module by automatically adding a corresponding LoadModule line to Apache's `httpd.conf` configuration file, or by enabling it if it already exists.

-A

> Same as option -a but the created LoadModule directive is prefixed with a hash sign (#), *i.e.*, the module is just prepared for later activation but initially disabled.

-e

> This indicates the editing operation, which can be used with the -a and -A options similarly to the -i operation to edit Apache's `httpd.conf` configuration file without attempting to install the module.

Examples

Assume you have an Apache module named mod_foo.c available which should extend Apache's server functionality. To accomplish this you first have to compile the C source into a shared object suitable for loading into the Apache server under runtime via the following command:

```
$ apxs -c mod_foo.c
/path/to/libtool --mode=compile gcc ... -c mod_foo.c
/path/to/libtool --mode=link gcc ... -o mod_foo.la mod_foo.slo
$ _
```

Then you have to update the Apache configuration by making sure a LoadModule directive is present to load this shared object. To simplify this step apxs provides an automatic way to install the shared object in its "modules" directory and updating the `httpd.conf` file accordingly. This can be achieved by running:

```
$ apxs -i -a mod_foo.la
/path/to/instdso.sh mod_foo.la /path/to/apache/modules
/path/to/libtool --mode=install cp mod_foo.la /path/to/apache/modules ... chmod 755
```

```
/path/to/apache/modules/mod_foo.so
[activating module `foo' in /path/to/apache/conf/httpd.conf]
$ _
```

This way a line named

```
LoadModule foo_module modules/mod_foo.so
```

is added to the configuration file if still not present. If you want to have this disabled per default use the -A option, *i.e.*

```
$ apxs -i -A mod_foo.c
```

For a quick test of the apxs mechanism you can create a sample Apache module template plus a corresponding Makefile via:

```
$ apxs -g -n foo
Creating [DIR]  foo
Creating [FILE] foo/Makefile
Creating [FILE] foo/modules.mk
Creating [FILE] foo/mod_foo.c
Creating [FILE] foo/.deps
$ _
```

Then you can immediately compile this sample module into a shared object and load it into the Apache server:

```
$ cd foo
$ make all reload
apxs -c mod_foo.c
/path/to/libtool --mode=compile gcc ... -c mod_foo.c
/path/to/libtool --mode=link gcc ... -o mod_foo.la mod_foo.slo
apxs -i -a -n "foo" mod_foo.la
/path/to/instdso.sh mod_foo.la /path/to/apache/modules
/path/to/libtool --mode=install cp mod_foo.la /path/to/apache/modules ... chmod 755
/path/to/apache/modules/mod_foo.so
[activating module `foo' in /path/to/apache/conf/httpd.conf]
apachectl restart
/path/to/apache/sbin/apachectl restart: httpd not running, trying to start
[Tue Mar 31 11:27:55 1998] [debug] mod_so.c(303): loaded module foo_module
/path/to/apache/sbin/apachectl restart: httpd started
$ _
```

Chapter 58.

configure - Configure the source tree

The `configure` script configures the source tree for compiling and installing the Apache HTTP Server on your particular platform. Various options allow the compilation of a server corresponding to your personal requirements.

This script, included in the root directory of the source distribution, is for compilation on Unix and Unix-like systems only. For other platforms, see the *platform* documentation.

Synopsis

You should call the `configure` script from within the root directory of the distribution.

`./configure` [*OPTION*] ... [*VAR=VALUE*] ...

To assign environment variables (e.g. CC, CFLAGS ...), specify them as *VAR=VALUE*. See *below* for descriptions of some of the useful variables.

Options

- *Configuration options*
- *Installation directories*
- *System types*
- *Optional features*
- *Options for support programs*

Configuration options

The following options influence the behavior of `configure` itself.

`-C`

`--config-cache`

This is an alias for `--cache-file=config.cache`

`--cache-file=`*FILE*

The test results will be cached in file *FILE*. This option is disabled by default.

-h

--help [short|recursive]

Output the help and exit. With the argument `short` only options specific to this package will displayed. The argument `recursive` displays the short help of all the included packages.

-n

--no-create

The `configure` script is run normally but does not create output files. This is useful to check the test results before generating makefiles for compilation.

-q

--quiet

Do not print `checking` ... messages during the configure process.

--srcdir=*DIR*

Defines directory *DIR* to be the source file directory. Default is the directory where `configure` is located, or the parent directory.

--silent

Same as `--quiet`

-v

--version

Display copyright information and exit.

Installation directories

These options define the installation directory. The installation tree depends on the selected layout.

--prefix=*PREFIX*

Install architecture-independent files in *PREFIX*. By default the installation directory is set to `/usr/local/apache2`.

--exec-prefix=*EPREFIX*

Install architecture-dependent files in *EPREFIX*. By default the installation directory is set to the *PREFIX* directory.

By default, `make install` will install all the files in `/usr/local/apache2/bin`, `/usr/local/apache2/lib` etc. You can specify an installation prefix other than `/usr/local/apache2` using `--prefix`, for instance `--prefix=$HOME`.

Define a directory layout

--enable-layout=*LAYOUT*

Configure the source code and build scripts to assume an installation tree based on the layout *LAYOUT*. This allows you to separately specify the locations for each type of file within the Apache HTTP Server installation. The `config.layout` file contains several example configurations, and you can also create your own custom configuration following the examples. The different layouts in this file are grouped into `<Layout FOO>...</Layout>` sections and referred to by name as in `FOO`. The default layout is `Apache`.

Fine tuning of the installation directories

For better control of the installation directories, use the options below. Please note that the directory defaults are set by `autoconf` and are overwritten by the corresponding layout setting.

--bindir=*DIR*

Install user executables in *DIR*. The user executables are supporting programs like *htpasswd*, *dbmmanage*, etc. which are useful for site administrators. By default *DIR* is set to *EPREFIX*/bin.

--datadir=*DIR*

Install read-only architecture-independent data in *DIR*. By default `datadir` is set to *PREFIX*/share. This option is offered by `autoconf` and currently unused.

--includedir=*DIR*

Install C header files in *DIR*. By default `includedir` is set to *EPREFIX*/include.

--infodir=*DIR*

Install info documentation in *DIR*. By default `infodir` is set to *PREFIX*/info. This option is currently unused.

--libdir=*DIR*

Install object code libraries in *DIR*. By default `libdir` is set to *EPREFIX*/lib.

--libexecdir=*DIR*

Install the program executables (i.e., shared modules) in *DIR*. By default `libexecdir` is set to *EPREFIX*/libexec.

--localstatedir=*DIR*

Install modifiable single-machine data in *DIR*. By default `localstatedir` is set to *PREFIX*/var. This option is offered by `autoconf` and currently unused.

--mandir=*DIR*

Install the man documentation in *DIR*. By default `mandir` is set to *EPREFIX*/`man`.

--oldincludedir=*DIR*

Install C header files for non-gcc in *DIR*. By default `oldincludedir` is set to `/usr/include`. This option is offered by `autoconf` and currently unused.

--sbindir=*DIR*

Install the system administrator executables in *DIR*. Those are server programs like `httpd, apachectl, suexec,` etc. which are neccessary to run the Apache HTTP Server. By default `sbindir` is set to *EPREFIX*/`sbin`.

--sharedstatedir=*DIR*

Install modifiable architecture-independent data in *DIR*. By default `sharedstatedir` is set to *PREFIX*/`com`. This option is offered by `autoconf` and currently unused.

--sysconfdir=*DIR*

Install read-only single-machine data like the server configuration files `httpd.conf`, `mime.types`, etc. in *DIR*. By default `sysconfdir` is set to *PREFIX*/`conf`.

System types

These options are used to cross-compile the Apache HTTP Server to run on another system. In normal cases, when building and running the server on the same system, these options are not used.

--build=*BUILD*

Defines the system type of the system on which the tools are being built. It defaults to the result of the script `config.guess`.

--host=*HOST*

Defines the system type of the system on which the server will run. *HOST* defaults to *BUILD.*

--target=*TARGET*

Configure for building compilers for the system type *TARGET*. It defaults to *HOST*. This option is offered by `autoconf` and not necessary for the Apache HTTP Server.

Optional Features

These options are used to fine tune the features your HTTP server will have.

General syntax

Generally you can use the following syntax to enable or disable a feature:

--disable-*FEATURE*

Do not include *FEATURE*. This is the same as `--enable-`*FEATURE*`=no`.

--enable-*FEATURE*[=*ARG*]

Include *FEATURE*. The default value for *ARG* is `yes`.

--enable-*MODULE*=shared

The corresponding module will be build as DSO module.

--enable-*MODULE*=static

By default enabled modules are linked statically. You can force this explicitly.

> **Note**
>
> `configure` will not complain about `--enable-`*foo* even if *foo* doesn't exist, so you need to type carefully.

Modules enabled by default

Some modules are compiled by default and have to be disabled explicitly. Use the following options to remove discrete modules from the compilation process.

--disable-actions

Disable action triggering on requests, which is provided by <u>mod_actions</u>.

--disable-alias

Disable the mapping of requests to different parts of the filesystem, which is provided by <u>mod_alias</u>.

--disable-asis

Disable support for as-is filetypes, which is provided by <u>mod_asis</u>.

--disable-auth

Disable user-based access control provided by <u>mod_auth</u>. This module provides for HTTP Basic Authentication, where the usernames and passwords are stored in plain text files.

--disable-autoindex

Disable the directory listing functionality provided by <u>mod_autoindex</u>.

--disable-access

Disable host-based access control provided by mod_access.

--disable-cgi

mod_cgi, which provides support for CGI scripts, is enabled by default when using a non-threaded MPM. Use this option to disable CGI support.

--disable-cgid

When using the threaded MPMs worker support for CGI scripts is provided by mod_cgid by default. To disable CGI support use this option.

--disable-charset-lite

Disable character set translation provided by mod_charset_lite. This module will be installed by default only on EBCDIC systems.

--disable-dir

Disable directory request handling provided by mod_dir.

--disable-env

Enable setting and clearing of environment variables, which is provided by mod_env.

--disable-http

Disable the HTTP protocol handling. The http module is a basic one, enabling the server to function as an HTTP server. It is only useful to disable it if you want to use another protocol module instead. **Don't disable this module unless you are really sure what you are doing.**
Note: This module will always be linked statically.

--disable-imagemap

Disable support for server based imagemaps, which provided by mod_imagemap.

--disable-include

Disable Server Side Includes provided by mod_include.

--disable-log-config

Disable the logging configuration provided by mod_log_config. You won't be able to log requests to the server without this module.

--disable-mime

mod_mime associates the requested filename's extensions with the file's behavior and content (*mime-type*, language, character set and encoding). Disabling this module is normally not recommended.

--disable-negotiation

Disable content negotiation provided by mod_negotiation.

--disable-setenvif

Disable support for basing environment variables on headers, which is provided by mod_setenvif.

--disable-status

Enable the process/thread monitoring, which is provided by mod_status.

--disable-userdir

Disable the mapping of requests to user-specific directories, which is provided by mod_userdir.

Modules, disabled by default

Some modules are compiled by default and have to be enabled explicitly or by using the keywords most or all (see --enable-mods-shared below for further explanation) to be available. Therefore use the options below.

--enable-auth-anon

Enable anonymous user access provided by mod_auth_anon.

--enable-auth-dbm

mod_auth_dbm provides for HTTP Basic Authentication, where the usernames and passwords are stored in DBM type database files. Use this option to enable the module.

--enable-auth-digest

Enable RFC2617 Digest authentication provided by mod_auth_digest. This module uses plain text files to store the credentials.

--enable-authnz-ldap

Enable LDAP based authentication provided by mod_authnz_ldap.

--enable-cache

Enable dynamic file caching provided by mod_cache. This experimental module may be interesting for servers with high load or caching proxy servers. At least one storage management module (e.g. mod_disk_cache or mod_mem_cache) is also necessary.

--enable-cern-meta

Enable the CERN-type meta files support provided by mod_cern_meta.

--enable-charset-lite

Enable character set translation provided by mod_charset_lite. This module will be installed by default only on EBCDIC systems. On other systems, you have to enable it.

--enable-dav

Enable the WebDAV protocol handling provided by mod_dav. Support for filesystem resources is provided by the separate module mod_dav_fs. This module is also automatically enabled with --enable-dav.
Note: mod_dav can only be used together with the http protocol module.

--enable-dav-fs

Enable DAV support for filesystem resources, which is provided by mod_dav_fs. This module is a provider for the mod_dav module, so you should also use --enable-dav.

--enable-dav-lock

Enable mod_dav_lock which provides generic DAV locking support for backend modules. This module needs at least mod_dav to function, so you should also use --enable-dav.

--enable-deflate

Enable deflate transfer encoding provided by mod_deflate.

--enable-disk-cache

Enable disk caching provided by mod_disk_cache.

--enable-expires

Enable Expires header control provided by mod_expires.

--enable-ext-filter

Enable the external filter support provided by mod_ext_filter.

--enable-file-cache

Enable the file cache provided by mod_file_cache.

--enable-headers

Enable control of HTTP headers provided by mod_headers.

--enable-info

Enable the server information provided by mod_info.

--enable-ldap

Enable LDAP caching and connection pooling services provided by mod_ldap.

--enable-logio

Enable logging of input and output bytes including headers provided by mod_logio.

--enable-mem-cache

Enable memory caching provided by mod_mem_cache.

--enable-mime-magic

Enable automatical determining of *MIME types*, which is provided by mod_mime_magic.

--enable-isapi

Enable the isapi extension support provided by mod_isapi.

--enable-proxy

Enable the proxy/gateway functionality provided by mod_proxy. The proxying capabilities for AJP13, CONNECT, FTP, HTTP and the balancer are provided by the separate modules mod_proxy_ajp, mod_proxy_connect, mod_proxy_ftp, mod_proxy_http and mod_proxy_balancer. These five modules are also automatically enabled with --enable-proxy.

--enable-proxy-ajp

Enable proxy support for AJP13 (Apache JServ Protocol 1.3) request handling, which is provided by mod_proxy_ajp. This module is an extension for the mod_proxy module, so you should also use --enable-proxy.

--enable-proxy-balancer

Enable load balancing support for the AJP13, FTP and HTTP protocols, which is provided by mod_proxy_balancer. This module is an extension for the mod_proxy module, so you should also use --enable-proxy.

--enable-proxy-connect

Enable proxy support for CONNECT request handling, which is provided by mod_proxy_connect. This module is an extension for the mod_proxy module, so you should also use --enable-proxy.

--enable-proxy-ftp

Enable proxy support for FTP requests, which is provided by mod_proxy_ftp. This module is an extension for the mod_proxy module, so you should also use --enable-proxy.

--enable-proxy-http

Enable proxy support for HTTP requests, which is provided by mod_proxy_http. This module is an extension for the mod_proxy module, so you should also use --enable-proxy.

--enable-rewrite

Enable rule based URL manipulation provided by mod_rewrite.

--enable-so

Enable DSO capability provided by mod_so. This module will be automatically enabled if you use the --enable-mods-shared option.

--enable-speling

Enable the functionality to correct common URL misspellings, which is provided by mod_speling.

--enable-ssl

Enable support for SSL/TLS provided by mod_ssl.

--enable-unique-id

Enable the generation of per-request unique ids, which is provided by mod_unique_id.

--enable-usertrack

Enable user-session tracking provided by mod_usertrack.

--enable-vhost-alias

Enable mass virtual hosting provided by mod_vhost_alias.

Modules for developers

The following modules are useful only for developers and testing purposes and are disabled by default. Use the following options to enable them. If you are not sure whether you need one of these modules, omit them.

--enable-bucketeer

Enable the manipulation filter for buckets, which is provided by mod_bucketeer.

--enable-case-filter

Enable the example uppercase conversion output filter support of mod_case_filter.

--enable-case-filter-in

Enable the example uppercase conversion input filter support of mod_case_filter_in.

--enable-echo

Enable the ECHO server provided by mod_echo.

--enable-example

Enable the example and demo module mod_example.

--enable-optional-fn-export

Enable the example for an optional function exporter, which is provided by mod_optional_fn_export.

--enable-optional-fn-import

Enable the example for an optional function importer, which is provided by mod_optional_fn_import.

--enable-optional-hook-export

Enable the example for an optional hook exporter, which is provided by mod_optional_hook_export.

--enable-optional-hook-import

Enable the example optional hook importer, which is provided by mod_optional_hook_import.

MPMs and third-party modules

To add the necessary Multi Processing Module and additional third-party modules use the following options:

--with-module=*module-type*:*module-file*[, *module-type*:*module-file*]

Add one or more third-party modules to the list of statically linked modules. The module source file *module-file* will be searched in the modules/*module-type* subdirectory of your Apache HTTP server source tree. If it is not found there configure is considering *module-file* to be an absolute file path and tries to copy the source file into the *module-type* subdirectory. If the subdirectory doesn't exist it will be created and populated with a standard Makefile.in.

This option is useful to add small external modules consisting of one source file. For more complex modules you should read the vendor's documentation.

 Note

If you want to build a DSO module instead of a statically linked use *apxs*.

--with-mpm=MPM

Choose the process model for your server. You have to select exactly one *Multi-Processing Module*. Otherwise the *default MPM* for your operating system will be taken. Possible MPMs are beos, mpmt_os2, prefork, and worker.

Cumulative and other options

--enable-maintainer-mode

Turn on debugging and compile time warnings.

--enable-mods-shared=*MODULE-LIST*

Defines a list of modules to be enabled and build as dynamic shared modules. This mean, these module have to be loaded dynamically by using the LoadModule directive.

MODULE-LIST is a space separated list of modulenames enclosed by quotation marks. The module names are given without the preceding mod_. For example:

```
--enable-mods-shared='headers rewrite dav'
```

Additionally you can use the special keywords all and most. For example,

```
--enable-mods-shared=most
```

will compile most modules and build them as DSO modules.

Caveat: --enable-mods-shared=all does not actually build all modules. To build all modules then, one might use:

```
./configure \
--with-ldap \
--enable-mods-shared="all ssl ldap cache proxy authn_alias mem_cache file_cache
authnz_ldap charset_lite dav_lock disk_cache"
```

--enable-modules=*MODULE-LIST*

This option behaves similar to --enable-mods-shared, but will link the given modules statically. This mean, these modules will always be present while running *httpd*. They need not be loaded with LoadModule.

--enable-v4-mapped

Allow IPv6 sockets to handle IPv4 connections.

--with-port=*PORT*

This defines the port on which *httpd* will listen. This port number is used when generating the configuration file httpd.conf. The default is 80.

--with-program-name

Define an alternative executable name. The default is httpd.

Optional packages

These options are used to define optional packages.

General syntax

Generally you can use the following syntax to define an optional package:

--with-*PACKAGE*[=*ARG*]

> Use the package *PACKAGE*. The default value for *ARG* is yes.

--without-*PACKAGE*

> Do not use the package *PACKAGE*. This is the same as --with-*PACKAGE*=no. This option is provided by autoconf but not very useful for the Apache HTTP Server.

Specific packages

--with-apr=*DIR*|*FILE*

> The *Apache Portable Runtime* (APR) is part of the httpd source distribution and will automatically be build together with the HTTP server. If you want to use an already installed APR instead you have to tell configure the path to the apr-config script. You may set the absolute path and name or the directory to the installed APR. apr-config must exist within this directory or the subdirectory bin.

--with-apr-util=*DIR*|*FILE*

> The Apache Portable Runtime Utilities (APU) are part of the httpd source distribution and will automatically be build together with the HTTP server. If you want to use an already installed APU instead you have to tell configure the path to the apu-config script. You may set the absolute path and name or the directory to the installed APU. apu-config must exist within this directory or the subdirectory bin.

--with-ssl=*DIR*

> If mod_ssl has been enabled configure searches for an installed OpenSSL. You can set the directory path to the SSL/TLS toolkit instead.

--with-z=*DIR*

> configure searches automatically for an installed zlib library if your source configuration requires one (e.g., when mod_deflate is enabled). You can set the directory path to the compression library instead.

Several features of the Apache HTTP Server, including mod_authn_dbm and mod_rewrite's DBM RewriteMap use simple key/value databases for quick lookups of information. SDBM is included in the APU, so this database is always available. If you would like to use other database types, use the following options to enable them:

--with-gdbm[=*path*]

If no *path* is specified, `configure` will search for the include files and libraries of a GNU DBM installation in the usual search paths. An explicit *path* will cause `configure` to look in *path*/`lib` and *path*/`include` for the relevant files. Finally, the *path* may specify specific include and library paths separated by a colon.

--with-ndbm[=*path*]

Like `--with-gdbm`, but searches for a New DBM installation.

--with-berkeley-db[=*path*]

Like `--with-gdbm`, but searches for a Berkeley DB installation.

Note

The DBM options are provided by the APU and passed through to its configuration script. They are useless when using an already installed APU defined by `--with-apr-util`.

You may use more then one DBM implementation together with your HTTP server. The appropriated DBM type will be configured within the runtime configuration at each time.

Options for support programs

--enable-static-support

Build a statically linked version of the support binaries. This means, a stand-alone executable will be built with all the necessary libraries integrated. Otherwise the support binaries are linked dynamically by default.

--enable-suexec

Use this option to enable *suexec*, which allows you to set uid and gid for spawned processes. **Do not use this option unless you understand all the security implications of running a suid binary on your server.** Further options to configure *suexec* are described *below*.

It is possible to create a statically linked binary of a single support program by using the following options:

--enable-static-ab

Build a statically linked version of *ab*.

--enable-static-checkgid

Build a statically linked version of `checkgid`.

--enable-static-htdbm

Build a statically linked version of *htdbm*.

--enable-static-htdigest

Build a statically linked version of *htdigest*.

--enable-static-htpasswd

Build a statically linked version of *htpasswd*.

--enable-static-logresolve

Build a statically linked version of *logresolve*.

--enable-static-rotatelogs

Build a statically linked version of *rotatelogs*.

suexec configuration options

The following options are used to fine tune the behavior of *suexec*. See *Configuring and installing suEXEC* for further information.

--with-suexec-bin

This defines the path to *suexec* binary. Default is --sbindir (see *Fine tuning of installation directories*).

--with-suexec-caller

This defines the user allowed to call *suexec*. It should be the same as the user under which *httpd* normally runs.

--with-suexec-docroot

This defines the directory tree under which *suexec* access is allowed for executables. Default value is --datadir/htdocs.

--with-suexec-gidmin

Define this as the lowest GID allowed to be a target user for *suexec*. The default value is 100.

--with-suexec-logfile

This defines the filename of the *suexec* logfile. By default the logfile is named suexec_log and located in --logfiledir.

--with-suexec-safepath

Define the value of the environment variable PATH to be set for processes started by *suexec*. Default value is /usr/local/bin:/usr/bin:/bin.

--with-suexec-userdir

This defines the subdirectory under the user's directory that contains all executables for which *suexec* access is allowed. This setting is necessary when you want to use *suexec* together with user-specific directories (as provided by <u>mod_userdir</u>). The default is public_html.

--with-suexec-uidmin

Define this as the lowest UID allowed to be a target user for *suexec*. The default value is 100.

--with-suexec-umask

Set umask for processes started by *suexec*. It defaults to your system settings.

Environment variables

There are some useful environment variables to override the choices made by configure or to help it to find libraries and programs with nonstandard names or locations.

CC

Define the C compiler command to be used for compilation.

CFLAGS

Set C compiler flags you want to use for compilation.

CPP

Define the C preprocessor command to be used.

CPPFLAGS

Set C/C++ preprocessor flags, e.g. -I*includedir* if you have headers in a nonstandard directory *includedir*.

LDFLAGS

Set linker flags, e.g. -L*libdir* if you have libraries in a nonstandard directory *libdir*.

Chapter 59.

dbmmanage - Manage user authentication files in DBM format

dbmmanage is used to create and update the DBM format files used to store usernames and password for basic authentication of HTTP users via mod_authn_dbm. Resources available from the Apache HTTP server can be restricted to just the users listed in the files created by dbmmanage. This program can only be used when the usernames are stored in a DBM file. To use a flat-file database see *htpasswd*.

This manual page only lists the command line arguments. For details of the directives necessary to configure user authentication in *httpd* see the httpd manual, which is part of the Apache distribution or can be found at *http://httpd.apache.org/*.

Synopsis

dbmmanage [*encoding*] *filename* add|adduser|check|delete|update *username* [*encpasswd* [*group* [,*group*...] [*comment*]]]

dbmmanage *filename* view [*username*]

dbmmanage *filename* import

Options

filename

> The filename of the DBM format file. Usually without the extension .db, .pag, or .dir.

username

> The user for which the operations are performed. The *username* may not contain a colon (:).

encpasswd

> This is the already encrypted password to use for the update and add commands. You may use a hyphen (-) if you want to get prompted for the password, but fill in the fields

afterwards. Additionally when using the update command, a period (.) keeps the original password untouched.

group

A group, which the user is member of. A groupname may not contain a colon (:). You may use a hyphen (-) if you don't want to assign the user to a group, but fill in the comment field. Additionally when using the update command, a period (.) keeps the original groups untouched.

comment

This is the place for your opaque comments about the user, like realname, mailaddress or such things. The server will ignore this field.

Encodings

-d

crypt encryption (default, except on Win32, Netware)

-m

MD5 encryption (default on Win32, Netware)

-s

SHA1 encryption

-p

plaintext (*not recommended*)

Commands

add

Adds an entry for *username* to *filename* using the encrypted password *encpasswd*.

```
dbmmanage passwords.dat add rbowen foKntnEF3KSXA
```

adduser

Asks for a password and then adds an entry for *username* to *filename*.

```
dbmmanage passwords.dat adduser krietz
```

check

Asks for a password and then checks if *username* is in *filename* and if it's password matches the specified one.

```
dbmmanage passwords.dat check rbowen
```

delete

Deletes the *username* entry from *filename*.

```
dbmmanage passwords.dat delete rbowen
```

import

Reads *username* : *password* entries (one per line) from STDIN and adds them to *filename*.
The passwords already have to be crypted.

update

Same as the adduser command, except that it makes sure *username* already exists in
filename.

```
dbmmanage passwords.dat update rbowen
```

view

Just displays the contents of the DBM file. If you specify a *username*, it displays the
particular record only.

```
dbmmanage passwords.dat view
```

Bugs

One should be aware that there are a number of different DBM file formats in existence, and
with all likelihood, libraries for more than one format may exist on your system. The three
primary examples are SDBM, NDBM, the GNU project's GDBM, and Berkeley DB 2.
Unfortunately, all these libraries use different file formats, and you must make sure that the
file format used by *filename* is the same format that dbmmanage expects to see. dbmmanage
currently has no way of determining what type of DBM file it is looking at. If used against
the wrong format, will simply return nothing, or may create a different DBM file with a
different name, or at worst, it may corrupt the DBM file if you were attempting to write to it.

dbmmanage has a list of DBM format preferences, defined by the @AnyDBM::ISA array near
the beginning of the program. Since we prefer the Berkeley DB 2 file format, the order in
which dbmmanage will look for system libraries is Berkeley DB 2, then NDBM, then GDBM
and then SDBM. The first library found will be the library dbmmanage will attempt to use
for all DBM file transactions. This ordering is slightly different than the standard
@AnyDBM::ISA ordering in Perl, as well as the ordering used by the simple dbmopen()
call in Perl, so if you use any other utilities to manage your DBM files, they must also follow
this preference ordering. Similar care must be taken if using programs in other languages,
like C, to access these files.

One can usually use the file program supplied with most Unix systems to see what format
a DBM file is in.

Chapter 60.
htcacheclean - Clean up the disk cache

htcacheclean is used to keep the size of mod_disk_cache's storage within a certain limit. This tool can run either manually or in daemon mode. When running in daemon mode, it sleeps in the background and checks the cache directories at regular intervals for cached content to be removed. You can stop the daemon cleanly by sending it a TERM or INT signal.

Synopsis

htcacheclean [-D] [-v] [-t] [-r] [-n] -p*path* -l*limit*
htcacheclean [-n] [-t] [-i] -d*interval* -p*path* -l*limit*

Options

-d*interval*

Daemonize and repeat cache cleaning every *interval* minutes. This option is mutually exclusive with the -D, -v and -r options. To shutdown the daemon cleanly, just send it a SIGTERM or SIGINT.

-D

Do a dry run and don't delete anything. This option is mutually exclusive with the -d option.

-v

Be verbose and print statistics. This option is mutually exclusive with the -d option.

-r

Clean thoroughly. This assumes that the Apache web server is not running (otherwise you may get garbage in the cache). This option is mutually exclusive with the -d option and implies the -t option.

-n

Be nice. This causes slower processing in favour of other processes. htcacheclean will sleep from time to time so that (a) the disk IO will be delayed and (b) the kernel can schedule other processes in the meantime.

-t

> Delete all empty directories. By default only cache files are removed, however with some configurations the large number of directories created may require attention. If your configuration requires a very large number of directories, to the point that inode or file allocation table exhaustion may become an issue, use of this option is advised.

-p*path*

> Specify *path* as the root directory of the disk cache. This should be the same value as specified with the `CacheRoot` directive.

-l*limit*

> Specify *limit* as the total disk cache size limit. The value is expressed in bytes by default (or attaching B to the number). Attach K for Kbytes or M for MBytes.

-i

> Be intelligent and run only when there was a modification of the disk cache. This option is only possible together with the `-d` option.

Exit Status

`htcacheclean` returns a zero status ("true") if all operations were successful, 1 otherwise.

Chapter 61.
htdbm - Manipulate DBM password databases

htdbm is used to manipulate the DBM format files used to store usernames and password for basic authentication of HTTP users via mod_authn_dbm. See the *dbmmanage* documentation for more information about these DBM files.

Synopsis

htdbm [-T*DBTYPE*] [-c] [-m | -d | -p | -s] [-t] [-v] [-x] *filename username*

htdbm -b [-T*DBTYPE*] [-c] [-m | -d | -p | -s] [-t] [-v] *filename username password*

htdbm -n [-c] [-m | -d | -p | -s] [-t] [-v] *username*

htdbm -nb [-c] [-m | -d | -p | -s] [-t] [-v] *username password*

htdbm -v [-T*DBTYPE*] [-c] [-m | -d | -p | -s] [-t] [-v] *filename username*

htdbm -vb [-T*DBTYPE*] [-c] [-m | -d | -p | -s] [-t] [-v] *filename username password*

htdbm -x [-T*DBTYPE*] [-m | -d | -p | -s] *filename username*

htdbm -l [-T*DBTYPE*]

Options

-b

> Use batch mode; *i.e.*, get the password from the command line rather than prompting for it. This option should be used with extreme care, since **the password is clearly visible** on the command line.

-c

> Create the *passwdfile*. If *passwdfile* already exists, it is rewritten and truncated. This option cannot be combined with the -n option.

-n

Display the results on standard output rather than updating a database. This option changes the syntax of the command line, since the *passwdfile* argument (usually the first one) is omitted. It cannot be combined with the -c option.

-m

Use MD5 encryption for passwords. On Windows, Netware and TPF, this is the default.

-d

Use crypt() encryption for passwords. The default on all platforms but Windows, Netware and TPF. Though possibly supported by htdbm on all platforms, it is not supported by the *httpd* server on Windows, Netware and TPF.

-s

Use SHA encryption for passwords. Facilitates migration from/to Netscape servers using the LDAP Directory Interchange Format (ldif).

-p

Use plaintext passwords. Though htdbm will support creation on all platforms, the *httpd* daemon will only accept plain text passwords on Windows, Netware and TPF.

-l

Print each of the usernames and comments from the database on stdout.

-t

Interpret the final parameter as a comment. When this option is specified, an additional string can be appended to the command line; this string will be stored in the "Comment" field of the database, associated with the specified username.

-v

Verify the username and password. The program will print a message indicating whether the supplied password is valid. If the password is invalid, the program exits with error code 3.

-x

Delete user. If the username exists in the specified DBM file, it will be deleted.

filename

The filename of the DBM format file. Usually without the extension .db, .pag, or .dir. If -c is given, the DBM file is created if it does not already exist, or updated if it does exist.

---

username

The username to create or update in *passwdfile*. If *username* does not exist in this file, an entry is added. If it does exist, the password is changed.

password

The plaintext password to be encrypted and stored in the DBM file. Used only with the -b flag.

-TDBTYPE

Type of DBM file (SDBM, GDBM, DB, or "default").

Bugs

One should be aware that there are a number of different DBM file formats in existence, and with all likelihood, libraries for more than one format may exist on your system. The three primary examples are SDBM, NDBM, GNU GDBM, and Berkeley/Sleepycat DB 2/3/4. Unfortunately, all these libraries use different file formats, and you must make sure that the file format used by *filename* is the same format that htdbm expects to see. htdbm currently has no way of determining what type of DBM file it is looking at. If used against the wrong format, will simply return nothing, or may create a different DBM file with a different name, or at worst, it may corrupt the DBM file if you were attempting to write to it.

One can usually use the file program supplied with most Unix systems to see what format a DBM file is in.

Exit Status

htdbm returns a zero status ("true") if the username and password have been successfully added or updated in the DBM File. htdbm returns 1 if it encounters some problem accessing files, 2 if there was a syntax problem with the command line, 3 if the password was entered interactively and the verification entry didn't match, 4 if its operation was interrupted, 5 if a value is too long (username, filename, password, or final computed record), 6 if the username contains illegal characters (see the *Restrictions section*), and 7 if the file is not a valid DBM password file.

Examples

```
htdbm /usr/local/etc/apache/.htdbm-users jsmith
```

Adds or modifies the password for user jsmith. The user is prompted for the password. If executed on a Windows system, the password will be encrypted using the modified Apache MD5 algorithm; otherwise, the system's crypt() routine will be used. If the file does not exist, htdbm will do nothing except return an error.

```
htdbm -c /home/doe/public_html/.htdbm jane
```

Creates a new file and stores a record in it for user jane. The user is prompted for the password. If the file exists and cannot be read, or cannot be written, it is not altered and htdbm will display a message and return an error status.

```
htdbm -mb /usr/web/.htdbm-all jones Pwd4Steve
```

Encrypts the password from the command line (Pwd4Steve) using the MD5 algorithm, and stores it in the specified file.

Security Considerations

Web password files such as those managed by htdbm should *not* be within the Web server's URI space -- that is, they should not be fetchable with a browser.

The use of the -b option is discouraged, since when it is used the unencrypted password appears on the command line.

Restrictions

On the Windows and MPE platforms, passwords encrypted with htdbm are limited to no more than 255 characters in length. Longer passwords will be truncated to 255 characters.

The MD5 algorithm used by htdbm is specific to the Apache software; passwords encrypted using it will not be usable with other Web servers.

Usernames are limited to 255 bytes and may not include the character :.

Chapter 62.

htdigest - manage user files for digest authentication

htdigest is used to create and update the flat-files used to store usernames, realm and password for digest authentication of HTTP users. Resources available from the Apache HTTP server can be restricted to just the users listed in the files created by htdigest.

This manual page only lists the command line arguments. For details of the directives necessary to configure digest authentication in *httpd* see the Apache manual, which is part of the Apache distribution or can be found at *http://httpd.apache.org/*.

Synopsis

htdigest [-c] *passwdfile realm username*

Options

-c

Create the *passwdfile*. If *passwdfile* already exists, it is deleted first.

passwdfile

Name of the file to contain the username, realm and password. If -c is given, this file is created if it does not already exist, or deleted and recreated if it does exist.

realm

The realm name to which the user name belongs.

username

The user name to create or update in *passwdfile*. If *username* does not exist is this file, an entry is added. If it does exist, the password is changed.

Security Considerations

This program is not safe as a setuid executable. Do *not* make it setuid.

Chapter 63.

htpasswd - Manage user files for basic authentication

htpasswd is used to create and update the flat-files used to store usernames and password for basic authentication of HTTP users. If htpasswd cannot access a file, such as not being able to write to the output file or not being able to read the file in order to update it, it returns an error status and makes no changes.

Resources available from the Apache HTTP server can be restricted to just the users listed in the files created by htpasswd. This program can only manage usernames and passwords stored in a flat-file. It can encrypt and display password information for use in other types of data stores, though. To use a DBM database see *dbmmanage*.

htpasswd encrypts passwords using either a version of MD5 modified for Apache, or the system's crypt() routine. Files managed by htpasswd may contain both types of passwords; some user records may have MD5-encrypted passwords while others in the same file may have passwords encrypted with crypt().

This manual page only lists the command line arguments. For details of the directives necessary to configure user authentication in *httpd* see the Apache manual, which is part of the Apache distribution or can be found at *http://httpd.apache.org/*.

Synopsis

```
htpasswd [ -c ] [ -m ] [ -D ] passwdfile username
htpasswd -b [ -c ] [ -m | -d | -p | -s ] [ -D ] passwdfile username password
htpasswd -n [ -m | -d | -s | -p ] username
htpasswd -nb [ -m | -d | -s | -p ] username password
```

Options

-b

> Use batch mode; *i.e.*, get the password from the command line rather than prompting for it. This option should be used with extreme care, since **the password is clearly visible** on the command line.

-c

Create the *passwdfile*. If *passwdfile* already exists, it is rewritten and truncated. This option cannot be combined with the -n option.

-n

Display the results on standard output rather than updating a file. This is useful for generating password records acceptable to Apache for inclusion in non-text data stores. This option changes the syntax of the command line, since the *passwdfile* argument (usually the first one) is omitted. It cannot be combined with the -c option.

-m

Use MD5 encryption for passwords. On Windows, Netware and TPF, this is the default.

-d

Use crypt() encryption for passwords. The default on all platforms but Windows, Netware and TPF. Though possibly supported by htpasswd on all platforms, it is not supported by the *httpd* server on Windows, Netware and TPF.

-s

Use SHA encryption for passwords. Facilitates migration from/to Netscape servers using the LDAP Directory Interchange Format (ldif).

-p

Use plaintext passwords. Though htpasswd will support creation on all platforms, the *httpd* daemon will only accept plain text passwords on Windows, Netware and TPF.

-D

Delete user. If the username exists in the specified htpasswd file, it will be deleted.

passwdfile

Name of the file to contain the user name and password. If -c is given, this file is created if it does not already exist, or rewritten and truncated if it does exist.

username

The username to create or update in *passwdfile*. If *username* does not exist in this file, an entry is added. If it does exist, the password is changed.

password

The plaintext password to be encrypted and stored in the file. Only used with the -b flag.

Exit Status

htpasswd returns a zero status ("true") if the username and password have been successfully added or updated in the *passwdfile*. htpasswd returns 1 if it encounters some problem accessing files, 2 if there was a syntax problem with the command line, 3 if the password was entered interactively and the verification entry didn't match, 4 if its operation was interrupted, 5 if a value is too long (username, filename, password, or final computed record), 6 if the username contains illegal characters (see the *Restrictions section*), and 7 if the file is not a valid password file.

Examples

```
htpasswd /usr/local/etc/apache/.htpasswd-users jsmith
```

Adds or modifies the password for user jsmith. The user is prompted for the password. If executed on a Windows system, the password will be encrypted using the modified Apache MD5 algorithm; otherwise, the system's crypt() routine will be used. If the file does not exist, htpasswd will do nothing except return an error.

```
htpasswd -c /home/doe/public_html/.htpasswd jane
```

Creates a new file and stores a record in it for user jane. The user is prompted for the password. If the file exists and cannot be read, or cannot be written, it is not altered and htpasswd will display a message and return an error status.

```
htpasswd -mb /usr/web/.htpasswd-all jones Pwd4Steve
```

Encrypts the password from the command line (Pwd4Steve) using the MD5 algorithm, and stores it in the specified file.

Security Considerations

Web password files such as those managed by htpasswd should *not* be within the Web server's URI space -- that is, they should not be fetchable with a browser.

This program is not safe as a setuid executable. Do *not* make it setuid.

The use of the -b option is discouraged, since when it is used the unencrypted password appears on the command line.

When using the crypt() algorithm, note that only the first 8 characters of the password are used to form the password. If the supplied password is longer, the extra characters will be silently discarded.

The SHA encryption format does not use salting: for a given password, there is only one encrypted representation. The crypt() and MD5 formats permute the representation by prepending a random salt string, to make dictionary attacks against the passwords more difficult.

Restrictions

On the Windows and MPE platforms, passwords encrypted with htpasswd are limited to no more than 255 characters in length. Longer passwords will be truncated to 255 characters.

The MD5 algorithm used by htpasswd is specific to the Apache software; passwords encrypted using it will not be usable with other Web servers.

Usernames are limited to 255 bytes and may not include the character :.

Chapter 64.

httxt2dbm - Generate dbm files for use with RewriteMap

httxt2dbm is used to generate dbm files from text input, for use in RewriteMap with the dbm map type.

Synopsis

httxt2dbm [-v] [-f *DBM_TYPE*] -i *SOURCE_TXT* -o *OUTPUT_DBM*

Options

-v

More verbose output

-f *DBM_TYPE*

Specify the DBM type to be used for the output. If not specified, will use the *APR* Default. Available types are:

GDBM for GDBM files
SDBM for SDBM files
DB for berkeley DB files
NDBM for NDBM files
default for the default DBM type

-i *SOURCE_TXT*

Input file from which the dbm is to be created. The file should be formated with one record per line, of the form:
key value
See the documentation for RewriteMap for further details of this file's format and meaning.

-o *OUTPUT_DBM*

Name of the output dbm files.

Examples

```
httxt2dbm -i rewritemap.txt -o rewritemap.dbm
httxt2dbm -f SDBM -i rewritemap.txt -o rewritemap.dbm
```

Chapter 65.

logresolve - Resolve IP-addresses to hostnames in Apache log files

logresolve is a post-processing program to resolve IP-addresses in Apache's access logfiles. To minimize impact on your nameserver, logresolve has its very own internal hash-table cache. This means that each IP number will only be looked up the first time it is found in the log file.

Takes an Apache log file on standard input. The IP addresses must be the first thing on each line and must be separated from the remainder of the line by a space.

Synopsis

logresolve [-s *filename*] [-c] < *access_log* > *access_log.new*

Options

-s *filename*

Specifies a filename to record statistics.

-c

This causes logresolve to apply some DNS checks: after finding the hostname from the IP address, it looks up the IP addresses for the hostname and checks that one of these matches the original address.

Chapter 66.

rotatelogs - Piped logging program to rotate Apache logs

rotatelogs is a simple program for use in conjunction with Apache's piped logfile feature. It supports rotation based on a time interval or maximum size of the log.

Synopsis

rotatelogs [-l] [-f] *logfile rotationtime|filesize*M [*offset*]

Options

`-l`

Causes the use of local time rather than GMT as the base for the interval or for strftime(3) formatting with size-based rotation. Note that using -l in an environment which changes the GMT offset (such as for BST or DST) can lead to unpredictable results!

`-f`

Causes the logfile to be opened immediately, as soon as rotatelogs starts, instead of waiting for the first logfile entry to be read (for non-busy sites, there may be a substantial delay between when the server is started and when the first request is handled, meaning that the associated logfile does not "exist" until then, which causes problems from some automated logging tools). *Available in version 2.2.9 and later.*

`logfile`

The path plus basename of the logfile. If *logfile* includes any '%' characters, it is treated as a format string for strftime(3). Otherwise, the suffix *.nnnnnnnnnn* is automatically added and is the time in seconds. Both formats compute the start time from the beginning of the current period. For example, if a rotation time of 86400 is specified, the hour, minute, and second fields created from the strftime(3) format will all be zero, referring to the beginning of the current 24-hour period (midnight).

`rotationtime`

The time between log file rotations in seconds. The rotation occurs at the beginning of this interval. For example, if the rotation time is 3600, the log file will be rotated at the beginning of every hour; if the rotation time is 86400, the log file will be rotated every night at midnight. (If no data is logged during an interval, no file will be created.)

`filesizeM`

The maximum file size in megabytes followed by the letter M to specify size rather than time.

`offset`

The number of minutes offset from UTC. If omitted, zero is assumed and UTC is used. For example, to use local time in the zone UTC -5 hours, specify a value of `-300` for this argument. In most cases, `-l` should be used instead of specifying an offset.

Examples

```
CustomLog "|bin/rotatelogs /var/logs/logfile 86400" common
```

This creates the files /var/logs/logfile.nnnn where nnnn is the system time at which the log nominally starts (this time will always be a multiple of the rotation time, so you can synchronize cron scripts with it). At the end of each rotation time (here after 24 hours) a new log is started.

```
CustomLog "|bin/rotatelogs -l /var/logs/logfile.%Y.%m.%d 86400" common
```

This creates the files /var/logs/logfile.yyyy.mm.dd where yyyy is the year, mm is the month, and dd is the day of the month. Logging will switch to a new file every day at midnight, local time.

```
CustomLog "|bin/rotatelogs /var/logs/logfile 5M" common
```

This configuration will rotate the logfile whenever it reaches a size of 5 megabytes.

```
ErrorLog "|bin/rotatelogs /var/logs/errorlog.%Y-%m-%d-%H_%M_%S 5M"
```

This configuration will rotate the error logfile whenever it reaches a size of 5 megabytes, and the suffix to the logfile name will be created of the form `errorlog.YYYY-mm-dd-HH_MM_SS`.

Portability

The following logfile format string substitutions should be supported by all `strftime(3)` implementations, see the `strftime(3)` man page for library-specific extensions.

%A	full weekday name (localized)
%a	3-character weekday name (localized)
%B	full month name (localized)
%b	3-character month name (localized)
%c	date and time (localized)
%d	2-digit day of month
%H	2-digit hour (24 hour clock)
%I	2-digit hour (12 hour clock)
%j	3-digit day of year
%M	2-digit minute
%m	2-digit month
%p	am/pm of 12 hour clock (localized)
%S	2-digit second
%U	2-digit week of year (Sunday first day of week)
%W	2-digit week of year (Monday first day of week)
%w	1-digit weekday (Sunday first day of week)
%X	time (localized)
%x	date (localized)
%Y	4-digit year
%y	2-digit year
%Z	time zone name
%%	literal `%'

Chapter 67.

suexec - Switch user before executing external programs

suexec is used by the Apache HTTP Server to switch to another user before executing CGI programs. In order to achieve this, it must run as root. Since the HTTP daemon normally doesn't run as root, the suexec executable needs the setuid bit set and must be owned by root. It should never be writable for any other person than root.

For further information about the concepts and and the security model of suexec please refer to the suexec documentation (*http://httpd.apache.org/docs/2.2/suexec.html*).

Synopsis

suexec -V

Options

-V

If you are root, this option displays the compile options of suexec. For security reasons all configuration options are changeable only at compile time.

Chapter 68.
Other Programs

The following programs are simple support programs included with the Apache HTTP Server which do not have their own manual pages. They are not installed automatically. You can find them after the configuration process in the support/ directory.

68.1. log_server_status

This perl script is designed to be run at a frequent interval by something like cron. It connects to the server and downloads the status information. It reformats the information to a single line and logs it to a file. Adjust the variables at the top of the script to specify the location of the resulting logfile.

68.2. split-logfile

This perl script will take a combined Web server access log file and break its contents into separate files. It assumes that the first field of each line is the virtual host identity (put there by "%v"), and that the logfiles should be named that + ".log" in the current directory.

The combined log file is read from stdin. Records read will be appended to any existing log files.

```
split-logfile < access_log
```

Part IX.

Apache Miscellaneous Documentation

Below is a list of additional documentation pages that apply to the Apache web server development project.

 Warning

The documents below have not been fully updated to take into account changes made in the 2.1 version of the Apache HTTP Server. Some of the information may still be relevant, but please use it with care.

Relevant Standards

This document acts as a reference page for most of the relevant standards that Apache follows.

Password Encryption Formats

Discussion of the various ciphers supported by Apache for authentication purposes.

Chapter 69.
Relevant Standards

This page documents all the relevant standards that the Apache HTTP Server follows, along with brief descriptions.

In addition to the information listed below, the following resources should be consulted:

- *http://purl.org/NET/http-errata* - HTTP/1.1 Specification Errata
- *http://www.rfc-editor.org/errata.html* - RFC Errata
- *http://ftp.ics.uci.edu/pub/ietf/http/#RFC* - A pre-compiled list of HTTP related RFCs

 Note

This document is not yet complete.

69.1. HTTP Recommendations

Regardless of what modules are compiled and used, Apache as a basic web server complies with the following IETF recommendations:

RFC 1945 **(Informational)**

The Hypertext Transfer Protocol (HTTP) is an application-level protocol with the lightness and speed necessary for distributed, collaborative, hypermedia information systems. This documents HTTP/1.0.

RFC 2616 **(Standards Track)**

The Hypertext Transfer Protocol (HTTP) is an application-level protocol for distributed, collaborative, hypermedia information systems. This documents HTTP/1.1.

RFC 2396 **(Standards Track)**

A Uniform Resource Identifier (URI) is a compact string of characters for identifying an abstract or physical resource.

69.2. HTML Recommendations

Regarding the Hypertext Markup Language, Apache complies with the following IETF and W3C recommendations:

RFC 2854 (Informational)[1]

This document summarizes the history of HTML development, and defines the "text/html" MIME type by pointing to the relevant W3C recommendations.

HTML 4.01 Specification (*Errata*)[2]

This specification defines the HyperText Markup Language (HTML), the publishing language of the World Wide Web. This specification defines HTML 4.01, which is a subversion of HTML 4.

HTML 3.2 Reference Specification[3]

The HyperText Markup Language (HTML) is a simple markup language used to create hypertext documents that are portable from one platform to another. HTML documents are SGML documents.

XHTML 1.1 - Module-based XHTML (*Errata*)[4]

This Recommendation defines a new XHTML document type that is based upon the module framework and modules defined in Modularization of XHTML.

XHTML 1.0 The Extensible HyperText Markup Language (Second Edition) (*Errata*)[5]

This specification defines the Second Edition of XHTML 1.0, a reformulation of HTML 4 as an XML 1.0 application, and three DTDs corresponding to the ones defined by HTML 4.

69.3. Authentication

Concerning the different methods of authentication, Apache follows the following IETF recommendations:

RFC 2617 (Draft standard)[6]

"HTTP/1.0", includes the specification for a Basic Access Authentication scheme.

69.4. Language/Country Codes

The following links document ISO and other language and country code information:

---

[1] *http://www.rfc-editor.org/rfc/rfc2854.txt*

[2] *http://www.w3.org/TR/html401*

[3] *http://www.w3.org/TR/REC-html32*

[4] *http://www.w3.org/2001/04/REC-xhtml-modularization-20010410-errata*

[5] *http://www.w3.org/TR/xhtml1*

[6] *http://www.rfc-editor.org/rfc/rfc2617.txt*

ISO 639-2[7]

ISO 639 provides two sets of language codes, one as a two-letter code set (639-1) and another as a three-letter code set (this part of ISO 639) for the representation of names of languages.

ISO 3166-1[8]

These pages document the country names (official short names in English) in alphabetical order as given in ISO 3166-1 and the corresponding ISO 3166-1-alpha-2 code elements.

BCP 47[9] (*Best Current Practice*), RFC 3066[10]

This document describes a language tag for use in cases where it is desired to indicate the language used in an information object, how to register values for use in this language tag, and a construct for matching such language tags.

RFC 3282[11] (Standards Track)

This document defines a "Content-language:" header, for use in cases where one desires to indicate the language of something that has RFC 822-like headers, like MIME body parts or Web documents, and an "Accept-Language:" header for use in cases where one wishes to indicate one's preferences with regard to language.

---

[7] *http://www.loc.gov/standards/iso639-2/*
[8] *http://www.iso.ch/iso/en/prods-services/iso3166ma/02iso-3166-code-lists/index.html*
[9] *http://www.rfc-editor.org/rfc/bcp/bcp47.txt*
[10] *http://www.rfc-editor.org/rfc/rfc3066.txt*
[11] *http://www.rfc-editor.org/rfc/rfc3282.txt*

Chapter 70.
Password Formats

Notes about the password encryption formats generated and understood by Apache.

70.1. Basic Authentication

There are four formats that Apache recognizes for basic-authentication passwords. Note that not all formats work on every platform:

PLAIN TEXT (i.e. *unencrypted*)

Windows, BEOS, & Netware only.

CRYPT

Unix only. Uses the traditional Unix crypt(3) function with a randomly-generated 32-bit salt (only 12 bits used) and the first 8 characters of the password.

SHA1

"{SHA}" + Base64-encoded SHA-1 digest of the password.

MD5

"$apr1$" + the result of an Apache-specific algorithm using an iterated (1,000 times) MD5 digest of various combinations of a random 32-bit salt and the password. See the APR source file *apr_md5.c*[1] for the details of the algorithm.

Generating values with htpasswd

MD5

```
$ htpasswd -nbm myName myPassword
myName:$apr1$r31.....$HqJZimcKQFAMYayBlzkrA/
```

SHA1

```
$ htpasswd -nbs myName myPassword
myName:{SHA}VBPuJHI7uixaa6LQGWx4s+5GKNE=
```

---

[1] *http://svn.apache.org/viewvc/apr/apr-util/branches/1.3.x/crypto/apr_md5.c?view=co*

CRYPT

```
$ htpasswd -nbd myName myPassword
myName:rqXexS6ZhobKA
```

Generating CRYPT and MD5 values with the OpenSSL command-line program

OpenSSL knows the Apache-specific MD5 algorithm.

MD5

```
$ openssl passwd -apr1 myPassword
$apr1$qHDFfhPC$nITSVHgYbDAK1Y0acGRnY0
```

CRYPT

```
openssl passwd -crypt myPassword
qQ5vTYO3c8dsU
```

Validating CRYPT or MD5 passwords with the OpenSSL command line program

The salt for a CRYPT password is the first two characters (converted to a binary value). To validate myPassword against rqXexS6ZhobKA

CRYPT

```
$ openssl passwd -crypt -salt rq myPassword
Warning: truncating password to 8 characters
rqXexS6ZhobKA
```

Note that using myPasswo instead of myPassword will produce the same result because only the first 8 characters of CRYPT passwords are considered.

The salt for an MD5 password is between $apr1$ and the following $ (as a Base64-encoded binary value - max 8 chars). To validate myPassword against $apr1$r31.....$HqJZimcKQFAMYayBlzkrA/

MD5

```
$ openssl passwd -apr1 -salt r31..... myPassword
$apr1$r31.....$HqJZimcKQFAMYayBlzkrA/
```

Database password fields for mod_dbd

The SHA1 variant is probably the most useful format for DBD authentication. Since the SHA1 and Base64 functions are commonly available, other software can populate a database with encrypted passwords that are usable by Apache basic authentication.

To create Apache SHA1-variant basic-authentication passwords in various languages:

PHP

```
'{SHA}' . base64_encode(sha1($password, TRUE))
```

Java

```
"{SHA}" + new
sun.misc.BASE64Encoder().encode(java.security.MessageDigest.getInstance("SHA1").dig
est(password.getBytes()))
```

ColdFusion

```
"{SHA}" & ToBase64(BinaryDecode(Hash(password, "SHA1"), "Hex"))
```

Ruby

```
require 'digest/sha1'
require 'base64'
'{SHA}' + Base64.encode64(Digest::SHA1.digest(password))
```

C or C++

```
Use the APR function: apr_sha1_base64
```

PostgreSQL (with the contrib/pgcrypto functions installed)

```
'{SHA}'||encode(digest(password,'sha1'),'base64')
```

70.2. Digest Authentication

Apache recognizes one format for digest-authentication passwords - the MD5 hash of the string `user:realm:password` as a 32-character string of hexadecimal digits. `realm` is the Authorization Realm argument to the AuthName directive in httpd.conf.

Database password fields for mod_dbd

Since the MD5 function is commonly available, other software can populate a database with encrypted passwords that are usable by Apache digest authentication.

To create Apache digest-authentication passwords in various languages:

PHP

```
md5($user . ':' . $realm . ':' .$password)
```

Java

```
byte b[] = java.security.MessageDigest.getInstance("MD5").digest( (user + ":" +
realm + ":" + password ).getBytes());
```

```
java.math.BigInteger bi = new java.math.BigInteger(1, b);
String s = bi.toString(16);
while (s.length() < 32)
s = "0" + s; // String s is the encrypted password
```

ColdFusion

```
LCase(Hash( (user & ":" & realm & ":" & password) , "MD5"))
```

Ruby

```
require 'digest/md5'
Digest::MD5.hexdigest(user + ':' + realm + ':' + password)
```

PostgreSQL (with the contrib/pgcrypto functions installed)

```
encode(digest( user || ':' || realm || ':' || password , 'md5'), 'hex')
```

Part X.

Developer Documentation for Apache 2.0

Many of the documents on these Developer pages are lifted from Apache 1.3's documentation. While they are all being updated to Apache 2.0, they are in different stages of progress. Please be patient, and point out any discrepancies or errors on the developer/ pages directly to the *dev@httpd.apache.org* mailing list.

Topics

- *Apache 1.3 API Notes*
- *Apache 2.0 Hook Functions*
- *Request Processing in Apache 2.0*
- *How filters work in Apache 2.0*
- *Converting Modules from Apache 1.3 to Apache 2.0*
- *Debugging Memory Allocation in APR*
- *Documenting Apache 2.0*
- *Apache 2.0 Thread Safety Issues*

External Resources

- Tools provided by Ian Holsman:
    - Apache 2 cross reference (*http://lxr.webperf.org/*)
    - Autogenerated Apache 2 code documentation (*http://docx.webperf.org/*)
- Module Development Tutorials by Kevin O'Donnell
    - Integrating a module into the Apache build system (*http://threebit.net/tutorials/apache2_modules/tut1/tutorial1.html*)
    - Handling configuration directives (*http://threebit.net/tutorials/apache2_modules/tut2/tutorial2.html*)
- Some notes on Apache module development by Ryan Bloom (*http://www.onlamp.com/pub/ct/38*)

- Developer articles at apachetutor (*http://www.apachetutor.org/*) include:
    - Request Processing in Apache (*http://www.apachetutor.org/dev/request*)
    - Configuration for Modules (*http://www.apachetutor.org/dev/config*)
    - Resource Management in Apache (*http://www.apachetutor.org/dev/pools*)
    - Connection Pooling in Apache (*http://www.apachetutor.org/dev/reslist*)
    - Introduction to Buckets and Brigades (*http://www.apachetutor.org/dev/brigades*)

Chapter 71.
Apache 1.3 API notes

 Warning

This document has not been updated to take into account changes made in the 2.0 version of the Apache HTTP Server. Some of the information may still be relevant, but please use it with care.

These are some notes on the Apache API and the data structures you have to deal with, *etc.* They are not yet nearly complete, but hopefully, they will help you get your bearings. Keep in mind that the API is still subject to change as we gain experience with it. (See the TODO file for what *might* be coming). However, it will be easy to adapt modules to any changes that are made. (We have more modules to adapt than you do).

A few notes on general pedagogical style here. In the interest of conciseness, all structure declarations here are incomplete -- the real ones have more slots that I'm not telling you about. For the most part, these are reserved to one component of the server core or another, and should be altered by modules with caution. However, in some cases, they really are things I just haven't gotten around to yet. Welcome to the bleeding edge.

Finally, here's an outline, to give you some bare idea of what's coming up, and in what order:

- *Basic concepts.*
  - *Handlers, Modules, and Requests*
  - *A brief tour of a module*
- *How handlers work*
  - *A brief tour of the request_rec*
  - *Where request_rec structures come from*
  - *Handling requests, declining, and returning error codes*
  - *Special considerations for response handlers*
  - *Special considerations for authentication handlers*
  - *Special considerations for logging handlers*
- *Resource allocation and resource pools*

- *Configuration, commands and the like*
  - *Per-directory configuration structures*
  - *Command handling*
  - *Side notes --- per-server configuration, virtual servers, etc.*

71.1. Basic concepts

We begin with an overview of the basic concepts behind the API, and how they are manifested in the code.

Handlers, Modules, and Requests

Apache breaks down request handling into a series of steps, more or less the same way the Netscape server API does (although this API has a few more stages than NetSite does, as hooks for stuff I thought might be useful in the future). These are:

- URI -> Filename translation

- Auth ID checking [is the user who they say they are?]

- Auth access checking [is the user authorized *here*?]

- Access checking other than auth

- Determining MIME type of the object requested

- `Fixups' -- there aren't any of these yet, but the phase is intended as a hook for possible extensions like `SetEnv`, which don't really fit well elsewhere.

- Actually sending a response back to the client.

- Logging the request

These phases are handled by looking at each of a succession of *modules*, looking to see if each of them has a handler for the phase, and attempting invoking it if so. The handler can typically do one of three things:

- *Handle* the request, and indicate that it has done so by returning the magic constant `OK`.

- *Decline* to handle the request, by returning the magic integer constant `DECLINED`. In this case, the server behaves in all respects as if the handler simply hadn't been there.

- Signal an error, by returning one of the HTTP error codes. This terminates normal handling of the request, although an ErrorDocument may be invoked to try to mop up, and it will be logged in any case.

Most phases are terminated by the first module that handles them; however, for logging, `fixups', and non-access authentication checking, all handlers always run (barring an error).

Also, the response phase is unique in that modules may declare multiple handlers for it, via a dispatch table keyed on the MIME type of the requested object. Modules may declare a response-phase handler which can handle *any* request, by giving it the key * / * (*i.e.*, a wildcard MIME type specification). However, wildcard handlers are only invoked if the server has already tried and failed to find a more specific response handler for the MIME type of the requested object (either none existed, or they all declined).

The handlers themselves are functions of one argument (a `request_rec` structure. vide infra), which returns an integer, as above.

A brief tour of a module

At this point, we need to explain the structure of a module. Our candidate will be one of the messier ones, the CGI module -- this handles both CGI scripts and the `ScriptAlias` config file command. It's actually a great deal more complicated than most modules, but if we're going to have only one example, it might as well be the one with its fingers in every place.

Let's begin with handlers. In order to handle the CGI scripts, the module declares a response handler for them. Because of `ScriptAlias`, it also has handlers for the name translation phase (to recognize `ScriptAlias`ed URIs), the type-checking phase (any `ScriptAlias`ed request is typed as a CGI script).

The module needs to maintain some per (virtual) server information, namely, the `ScriptAlias`es in effect; the module structure therefore contains pointers to a functions which builds these structures, and to another which combines two of them (in case the main server and a virtual server both have `ScriptAlias`es declared).

Finally, this module contains code to handle the `ScriptAlias` command itself. This particular module only declares one command, but there could be more, so modules have *command tables* which declare their commands, and describe where they are permitted, and how they are to be invoked.

A final note on the declared types of the arguments of some of these commands: a `pool` is a pointer to a *resource pool* structure; these are used by the server to keep track of the memory which has been allocated, files opened, *etc.*, either to service a particular request, or to handle the process of configuring itself. That way, when the request is over (or, for the configuration pool, when the server is restarting), the memory can be freed, and the files closed, *en masse*, without anyone having to write explicit code to track them all down and dispose of them. Also, a `cmd_parms` structure contains various information about the config file being read, and other status information, which is sometimes of use to the function which processes a config-file command (such as `ScriptAlias`). With no further ado, the module itself:

```
/* Declarations of handlers. */

int translate_scriptalias (request_rec *);
int type_scriptalias (request_rec *);
int cgi_handler (request_rec *);

/* Subsidiary dispatch table for response-phase
 * handlers, by MIME type */

handler_rec cgi_handlers[] = {
{ "application/x-httpd-cgi", cgi_handler },
{ NULL }
};

/* Declarations of routines to manipulate the
 * module's configuration info. Note that these are
 * returned, and passed in, as void *'s; the server
 * core keeps track of them, but it doesn't, and can't,
 * know their internal structure.
 */

void *make_cgi_server_config (pool *);
void *merge_cgi_server_config (pool *, void *, void *);

/* Declarations of routines to handle config-file commands */

extern char *script_alias(cmd_parms *, void *per_dir_config, char *fake, char
*real);

command_rec cgi_cmds[] = {
{ "ScriptAlias", script_alias, NULL, RSRC_CONF, TAKE2,
"a fakename and a realname"},
{ NULL }
};

module cgi_module = {
  STANDARD_MODULE_STUFF,
  NULL,                     /* initializer */
  NULL,                     /* dir config creator */
  NULL,                     /* dir merger */
  make_cgi_server_config,   /* server config */
  merge_cgi_server_config,  /* merge server config */
  cgi_cmds,                 /* command table */
  cgi_handlers,             /* handlers */
  translate_scriptalias,    /* filename translation */
  NULL,                     /* check_user_id */
  NULL,                     /* check auth */
  NULL,                     /* check access */
  type_scriptalias,         /* type_checker */
  NULL,                     /* fixups */
  NULL,                     /* logger */
  NULL                      /* header parser */
};
```

71.2. How handlers work

The sole argument to handlers is a `request_rec` structure. This structure describes a particular request which has been made to the server, on behalf of a client. In most cases, each connection to the client generates only one `request_rec` structure.

A brief tour of the request_rec

The `request_rec` contains pointers to a resource pool which will be cleared when the server is finished handling the request; to structures containing per-server and per-connection information, and most importantly, information on the request itself.

The most important such information is a small set of character strings describing attributes of the object being requested, including its URI, filename, content-type and content-encoding (these being filled in by the translation and type-check handlers which handle the request, respectively).

Other commonly used data items are tables giving the MIME headers on the client's original request, MIME headers to be sent back with the response (which modules can add to at will), and environment variables for any subprocesses which are spawned off in the course of servicing the request. These tables are manipulated using the `ap_table_get` and `ap_table_set` routines.

> Note that the `Content-type` header value *cannot* be set by module content-handlers using the `ap_table_*()` routines. Rather, it is set by pointing the `content_type` field in the `request_rec` structure to an appropriate string. *e.g.*,
>
> `r->content_type = "text/html";`

Finally, there are pointers to two data structures which, in turn, point to per-module configuration structures. Specifically, these hold pointers to the data structures which the module has built to describe the way it has been configured to operate in a given directory (via `.htaccess` files or `<Directory>` sections), for private data it has built in the course of servicing the request (so modules' handlers for one phase can pass `notes' to their handlers for other phases). There is another such configuration vector in the `server_rec` data structure pointed to by the `request_rec`, which contains per (virtual) server configuration data.

Here is an abridged declaration, giving the fields most commonly used:

```
struct request_rec {

pool *pool;
conn_rec *connection;
server_rec *server;
```

```
/* What object is being requested */

char *uri;
char *filename;
char *path_info;
char *args;              /* QUERY_ARGS, if any */
struct stat finfo;       /* Set by server core;
                          * st_mode set to zero if no such file */
char *content_type;
char *content_encoding;

/* MIME header environments, in and out. Also,
 * an array containing environment variables to
 * be passed to subprocesses, so people can write
 * modules to add to that environment.
 *
 * The difference between headers_out and
 * err_headers_out is that the latter are printed
 * even on error, and persist across internal
 * redirects (so the headers printed for
 * ErrorDocument handlers will have them).
 */

table *headers_in;
table *headers_out;
table *err_headers_out;
table *subprocess_env;

/* Info about the request itself... */
int header_only;        /* HEAD request, as opposed to GET */
char *protocol;         /* Protocol, as given to us, or HTTP/0.9 */
char *method;           /* GET, HEAD, POST, etc. */
int method_number;      /* M_GET, M_POST, etc. */

/* Info for logging */

char *the_request;
int bytes_sent;

/* A flag which modules can set, to indicate that
 * the data being returned is volatile, and clients
 * should be told not to cache it.
 */

int no_cache;

/* Various other config info which may change
 * with .htaccess files
 * These are config vectors, with one void*
 * pointer for each module (the thing pointed
 * to being the module's business).
 */
void *per_dir_config;    /* Options set in config files, etc. */
```

```
void *request_config;    /* Notes on *this* request */

};
```

Where request_rec structures come from

Most request_rec structures are built by reading an HTTP request from a client, and filling in the fields. However, there are a few exceptions:

- If the request is to an imagemap, a type map (*i.e.*, a * . var file), or a CGI script which returned a local `Location:', then the resource which the user requested is going to be ultimately located by some URI other than what the client originally supplied. In this case, the server does an *internal redirect*, constructing a new request_rec for the new URI, and processing it almost exactly as if the client had requested the new URI directly.

- If some handler signaled an error, and an ErrorDocument is in scope, the same internal redirect machinery comes into play.

- Finally, a handler occasionally needs to investigate `what would happen if' some other request were run. For instance, the directory indexing module needs to know what MIME type would be assigned to a request for each directory entry, in order to figure out what icon to use.

  Such handlers can construct a *sub-request*, using the functions ap_sub_req_lookup_file, ap_sub_req_lookup_uri, and ap_sub_req_method_uri; these construct a new request_rec structure and processes it as you would expect, up to but not including the point of actually sending a response. (These functions skip over the access checks if the sub-request is for a file in the same directory as the original request).

  (Server-side includes work by building sub-requests and then actually invoking the response handler for them, via the function ap_run_sub_req).

Handling requests, declining, and returning error codes

As discussed above, each handler, when invoked to handle a particular request_rec, has to return an int to indicate what happened. That can either be

- OK -- the request was handled successfully. This may or may not terminate the phase.

- DECLINED -- no erroneous condition exists, but the module declines to handle the phase; the server tries to find another.

- an HTTP error code, which aborts handling of the request.

Note that if the error code returned is REDIRECT, then the module should put a Location in the request's headers_out, to indicate where the client should be redirected *to*.

Special considerations for response handlers

Handlers for most phases do their work by simply setting a few fields in the request_rec structure (or, in the case of access checkers, simply by returning the correct error code). However, response handlers have to actually send a request back to the client.

They should begin by sending an HTTP response header, using the function ap_send_http_header. (You don't have to do anything special to skip sending the header for HTTP/0.9 requests; the function figures out on its own that it shouldn't do anything). If the request is marked header_only, that's all they should do; they should return after that, without attempting any further output.

Otherwise, they should produce a request body which responds to the client as appropriate. The primitives for this are ap_rputc and ap_rprintf, for internally generated output, and ap_send_fd, to copy the contents of some FILE * straight to the client.

At this point, you should more or less understand the following piece of code, which is the handler which handles GET requests which have no more specific handler; it also shows how conditional GETs can be handled, if it's desirable to do so in a particular response handler -- ap_set_last_modified checks against the If-modified-since value supplied by the client, if any, and returns an appropriate code (which will, if nonzero, be USE_LOCAL_COPY). No similar considerations apply for ap_set_content_length, but it returns an error code for symmetry.

```
int default_handler (request_rec *r)
{
int errstatus;
FILE *f;

if (r->method_number != M_GET) return DECLINED;
if (r->finfo.st_mode == 0) return NOT_FOUND;

if ((errstatus = ap_set_content_length (r, r->finfo.st_size))
    || (errstatus = ap_set_last_modified (r, r->finfo.st_mtime)))
return errstatus;

f = fopen (r->filename, "r");

if (f == NULL) {
log_reason("file permissions deny server access", r->filename, r);
return FORBIDDEN;
}

register_timeout ("send", r);
```

```
ap_send_http_header (r);

if (!r->header_only) send_fd (f, r);
ap_pfclose (r->pool, f);
return OK;
}
```

Finally, if all of this is too much of a challenge, there are a few ways out of it. First off, as shown above, a response handler which has not yet produced any output can simply return an error code, in which case the server will automatically produce an error response. Secondly, it can punt to some other handler by invoking ap_internal_redirect, which is how the internal redirection machinery discussed above is invoked. A response handler which has internally redirected should always return OK.

(Invoking ap_internal_redirect from handlers which are *not* response handlers will lead to serious confusion).

Special considerations for authentication handlers

Stuff that should be discussed here in detail:

- Authentication-phase handlers not invoked unless auth is configured for the directory.
- Common auth configuration stored in the core per-dir configuration; it has accessors ap_auth_type, ap_auth_name, and ap_requires.
- Common routines, to handle the protocol end of things, at least for HTTP basic authentication (ap_get_basic_auth_pw, which sets the connection->user structure field automatically, and ap_note_basic_auth_failure, which arranges for the proper WWW-Authenticate: header to be sent back).

Special considerations for logging handlers

When a request has internally redirected, there is the question of what to log. Apache handles this by bundling the entire chain of redirects into a list of request_rec structures which are threaded through the r->prev and r->next pointers. The request_rec which is passed to the logging handlers in such cases is the one which was originally built for the initial request from the client; note that the bytes_sent field will only be correct in the last request in the chain (the one for which a response was actually sent).

71.3. Resource allocation and resource pools

One of the problems of writing and designing a server-pool server is that of preventing leakage, that is, allocating resources (memory, open files, *etc.*), without subsequently releasing them. The resource pool machinery is designed to make it easy to prevent this from happening, by allowing resource to be allocated in such a way that they are *automatically* released when the server is done with them.

The way this works is as follows: the memory which is allocated, file opened, *etc.*, to deal with a particular request are tied to a *resource pool* which is allocated for the request. The pool is a data structure which itself tracks the resources in question.

When the request has been processed, the pool is *cleared*. At that point, all the memory associated with it is released for reuse, all files associated with it are closed, and any other clean-up functions which are associated with the pool are run. When this is over, we can be confident that all the resource tied to the pool have been released, and that none of them have leaked.

Server restarts, and allocation of memory and resources for per-server configuration, are handled in a similar way. There is a *configuration pool*, which keeps track of resources which were allocated while reading the server configuration files, and handling the commands therein (for instance, the memory that was allocated for per-server module configuration, log files and other files that were opened, and so forth). When the server restarts, and has to reread the configuration files, the configuration pool is cleared, and so the memory and file descriptors which were taken up by reading them the last time are made available for reuse.

It should be noted that use of the pool machinery isn't generally obligatory, except for situations like logging handlers, where you really need to register cleanups to make sure that the log file gets closed when the server restarts (this is most easily done by using the function *ap_pfopen*, which also arranges for the underlying file descriptor to be closed before any child processes, such as for CGI scripts, are execed), or in case you are using the timeout machinery (which isn't yet even documented here). However, there are two benefits to using it: resources allocated to a pool never leak (even if you allocate a scratch string, and just forget about it); also, for memory allocation, `ap_palloc` is generally faster than `malloc`.

We begin here by describing how memory is allocated to pools, and then discuss how other resources are tracked by the resource pool machinery.

Allocation of memory in pools

Memory is allocated to pools by calling the function `ap_palloc`, which takes two arguments, one being a pointer to a resource pool structure, and the other being the amount of memory to allocate (in `chars`). Within handlers for handling requests, the most common way of getting a resource pool structure is by looking at the `pool` slot of the relevant `request_rec`; hence the repeated appearance of the following idiom in module code:

```
int my_handler(request_rec *r)
{
struct my_structure *foo;
...

foo = (foo *)ap_palloc (r->pool, sizeof(my_structure));
}
```

Note that *there is no ap_pfree* -- ap_palloced memory is freed only when the associated resource pool is cleared. This means that ap_palloc does not have to do as much accounting as malloc(); all it does in the typical case is to round up the size, bump a pointer, and do a range check.

(It also raises the possibility that heavy use of ap_palloc could cause a server process to grow excessively large. There are two ways to deal with this, which are dealt with below; briefly, you can use malloc, and try to be sure that all of the memory gets explicitly freed, or you can allocate a sub-pool of the main pool, allocate your memory in the sub-pool, and clear it out periodically. The latter technique is discussed in the section on sub-pools below, and is used in the directory-indexing code, in order to avoid excessive storage allocation when listing directories with thousands of files).

71.3.1. Allocating initialized memory

There are functions which allocate initialized memory, and are frequently useful. The function ap_pcalloc has the same interface as ap_palloc, but clears out the memory it allocates before it returns it. The function ap_pstrdup takes a resource pool and a char * as arguments, and allocates memory for a copy of the string the pointer points to, returning a pointer to the copy. Finally ap_pstrcat is a varargs-style function, which takes a pointer to a resource pool, and at least two char * arguments, the last of which must be NULL. It allocates enough memory to fit copies of each of the strings, as a unit; for instance:

```
ap_pstrcat (r->pool, "foo", "/", "bar", NULL);
```

returns a pointer to 8 bytes worth of memory, initialized to "foo/bar".

Commonly-used pools in the Apache Web server

A pool is really defined by its lifetime more than anything else. There are some static pools in http_main which are passed to various non-http_main functions as arguments at opportune times. Here they are:

permanent_pool

- never passed to anything else, this is the ancestor of all pools

pconf

- subpool of permanent_pool

- created at the beginning of a config "cycle"; exists until the server is terminated or restarts; passed to all config-time routines, either via cmd->pool, or as the "pool *p" argument on those which don't take pools
- passed to the module init() functions

ptemp

- sorry I lie, this pool isn't called this currently in 1.3, I renamed it this in my pthreads development. I'm referring to the use of ptrans in the parent... contrast this with the later definition of ptrans in the child.
- subpool of permanent_pool
- created at the beginning of a config "cycle"; exists until the end of config parsing; passed to config-time routines *via* cmd->temp_pool. Somewhat of a "bastard child" because it isn't available everywhere. Used for temporary scratch space which may be needed by some config routines but which is deleted at the end of config.

pchild

- subpool of permanent_pool
- created when a child is spawned (or a thread is created); lives until that child (thread) is destroyed
- passed to the module child_init functions
- destruction happens right after the child_exit functions are called... (which may explain why I think child_exit is redundant and unneeded)

ptrans

- should be a subpool of pchild, but currently is a subpool of permanent_pool, see above
- cleared by the child before going into the accept() loop to receive a connection
- used as connection->pool

r->pool

- for the main request this is a subpool of connection->pool; for subrequests it is a subpool of the parent request's pool.
- exists until the end of the request (*i.e.*, ap_destroy_sub_req, or in child_main after process_request has finished)
- note that r itself is allocated from r->pool; *i.e.*, r->pool is first created and then r is the first thing palloc()d from it

For almost everything folks do, r->pool is the pool to use. But you can see how other lifetimes, such as pchild, are useful to some modules... such as modules that need to open a database connection once per child, and wish to clean it up when the child dies.

You can also see how some bugs have manifested themself, such as setting connection->user to a value from r->pool -- in this case connection exists for the lifetime of ptrans, which is longer than r->pool (especially if r->pool is a subrequest!). So the correct thing to do is to allocate from connection->pool.

And there was another interesting bug in mod_include / mod_cgi. You'll see in those that they do this test to decide if they should use r->pool or r->main->pool. In this case the resource that they are registering for cleanup is a child process. If it were registered in r->pool, then the code would wait() for the child when the subrequest finishes. With mod_include this could be any old #include, and the delay can be up to 3 seconds... and happened quite frequently. Instead the subprocess is registered in r->main->pool which causes it to be cleaned up when the entire request is done -- *i.e.*, after the output has been sent to the client and logging has happened.

71.4. Tracking open files, etc.

As indicated above, resource pools are also used to track other sorts of resources besides memory. The most common are open files. The routine which is typically used for this is ap_pfopen, which takes a resource pool and two strings as arguments; the strings are the same as the typical arguments to fopen, *e.g.*,

```
...
FILE *f = ap_pfopen (r->pool, r->filename, "r");

if (f == NULL) { ... } else { ... }
```

There is also a ap_popenf routine, which parallels the lower-level open system call. Both of these routines arrange for the file to be closed when the resource pool in question is cleared.

Unlike the case for memory, there *are* functions to close files allocated with ap_pfopen, and ap_popenf, namely ap_pfclose and ap_pclosef. (This is because, on many systems, the number of files which a single process can have open is quite limited). It is important to use these functions to close files allocated with ap_pfopen and ap_popenf, since to do otherwise could cause fatal errors on systems such as Linux, which react badly if the same FILE* is closed more than once.

(Using the close functions is not mandatory, since the file will eventually be closed regardless, but you should consider it in cases where your module is opening, or could open, a lot of files).

Other sorts of resources -- cleanup functions

More text goes here. Describe the cleanup primitives in terms of which the file stuff is implemented; also, `spawn_process`.

Pool cleanups live until `clear_pool()` is called: `clear_pool(a)` recursively calls `destroy_pool()` on all subpools of a; then calls all the cleanups for a; then releases all the memory for a. `destroy_pool(a)` calls `clear_pool(a)` and then releases the pool structure itself. *i.e.,* `clear_pool(a)` doesn't delete a, it just frees up all the resources and you can start using it again immediately.

Fine control -- creating and dealing with sub-pools, with a note on sub-requests

On rare occasions, too-free use of `ap_palloc()` and the associated primitives may result in undesirably profligate resource allocation. You can deal with such a case by creating a *sub-pool*, allocating within the sub-pool rather than the main pool, and clearing or destroying the sub-pool, which releases the resources which were associated with it. (This really *is* a rare situation; the only case in which it comes up in the standard module set is in case of listing directories, and then only with *very* large directories. Unnecessary use of the primitives discussed here can hair up your code quite a bit, with very little gain).

The primitive for creating a sub-pool is `ap_make_sub_pool`, which takes another pool (the parent pool) as an argument. When the main pool is cleared, the sub-pool will be destroyed. The sub-pool may also be cleared or destroyed at any time, by calling the functions `ap_clear_pool` and `ap_destroy_pool`, respectively. (The difference is that `ap_clear_pool` frees resources associated with the pool, while `ap_destroy_pool` also deallocates the pool itself. In the former case, you can allocate new resources within the pool, and clear it again, and so forth; in the latter case, it is simply gone).

One final note -- sub-requests have their own resource pools, which are sub-pools of the resource pool for the main request. The polite way to reclaim the resources associated with a sub request which you have allocated (using the `ap_sub_req_ . . .` functions) is `ap_destroy_sub_req`, which frees the resource pool. Before calling this function, be sure to copy anything that you care about which might be allocated in the sub-request's resource pool into someplace a little less volatile (for instance, the filename in its `request_rec` structure).

(Again, under most circumstances, you shouldn't feel obliged to call this function; only 2K of memory or so are allocated for a typical sub request, and it will be freed anyway when the main request pool is cleared. It is only when you are allocating many, many sub-requests for a single main request that you should seriously consider the `ap_destroy_ . . .` functions).

71.5. Configuration, commands and the like

One of the design goals for this server was to maintain external compatibility with the NCSA 1.3 server --- that is, to read the same configuration files, to process all the directives therein correctly, and in general to be a drop-in replacement for NCSA. On the other hand, another design goal was to move as much of the server's functionality into modules which have as little as possible to do with the monolithic server core. The only way to reconcile these goals is to move the handling of most commands from the central server into the modules.

However, just giving the modules command tables is not enough to divorce them completely from the server core. The server has to remember the commands in order to act on them later. That involves maintaining data which is private to the modules, and which can be either per-server, or per-directory. Most things are per-directory, including in particular access control and authorization information, but also information on how to determine file types from suffixes, which can be modified by AddType and DefaultType directives, and so forth. In general, the governing philosophy is that anything which *can* be made configurable by directory should be; per-server information is generally used in the standard set of modules for information like Aliases and Redirects which come into play before the request is tied to a particular place in the underlying file system.

Another requirement for emulating the NCSA server is being able to handle the per-directory configuration files, generally called .htaccess files, though even in the NCSA server they can contain directives which have nothing at all to do with access control. Accordingly, after URI -> filename translation, but before performing any other phase, the server walks down the directory hierarchy of the underlying filesystem, following the translated pathname, to read any .htaccess files which might be present. The information which is read in then has to be *merged* with the applicable information from the server's own config files (either from the <Directory> sections in access.conf, or from defaults in srm.conf, which actually behaves for most purposes almost exactly like <Directory />).

Finally, after having served a request which involved reading .htaccess files, we need to discard the storage allocated for handling them. That is solved the same way it is solved wherever else similar problems come up, by tying those structures to the per-transaction resource pool.

Per-directory configuration structures

Let's look out how all of this plays out in mod_mime.c, which defines the file typing handler which emulates the NCSA server's behavior of determining file types from suffixes. What we'll be looking at, here, is the code which implements the AddType and

AddEncoding commands. These commands can appear in .htaccess files, so they must be handled in the module's private per-directory data, which in fact, consists of two separate tables for MIME types and encoding information, and is declared as follows:

```
typedef struct {
    table *forced_types;      /* Additional AddTyped stuff */
    table *encoding_types;    /* Added with AddEncoding... */
} mime_dir_config;
```

When the server is reading a configuration file, or <Directory> section, which includes one of the MIME module's commands, it needs to create a mime_dir_config structure, so those commands have something to act on. It does this by invoking the function it finds in the module's `create per-dir config slot', with two arguments: the name of the directory to which this configuration information applies (or NULL for srm.conf), and a pointer to a resource pool in which the allocation should happen.

(If we are reading a .htaccess file, that resource pool is the per-request resource pool for the request; otherwise it is a resource pool which is used for configuration data, and cleared on restarts. Either way, it is important for the structure being created to vanish when the pool is cleared, by registering a cleanup on the pool if necessary).

For the MIME module, the per-dir config creation function just ap_pallocs the structure above, and a creates a couple of tables to fill it. That looks like this:

```
void *create_mime_dir_config (pool *p, char *dummy)
{
mime_dir_config *new =
(mime_dir_config *) ap_palloc (p, sizeof(mime_dir_config));

new->forced_types = ap_make_table (p, 4);
new->encoding_types = ap_make_table (p, 4);

return new;
}
```

Now, suppose we've just read in a .htaccess file. We already have the per-directory configuration structure for the next directory up in the hierarchy. If the .htaccess file we just read in didn't have any AddType or AddEncoding commands, its per-directory config structure for the MIME module is still valid, and we can just use it. Otherwise, we need to merge the two structures somehow.

To do that, the server invokes the module's per-directory config merge function, if one is present. That function takes three arguments: the two structures being merged, and a resource pool in which to allocate the result. For the MIME module, all that needs to be done is overlay the tables from the new per-directory config structure with those from the parent:

```
void *merge_mime_dir_configs (pool *p, void *parent_dirv, void *subdirv)
{
mime_dir_config *parent_dir = (mime_dir_config *)parent_dirv;
mime_dir_config *subdir = (mime_dir_config *)subdirv;
mime_dir_config *new =
(mime_dir_config *)ap_palloc (p, sizeof(mime_dir_config));

new->forced_types = ap_overlay_tables (p, subdir->forced_types,
parent_dir->forced_types);
new->encoding_types = ap_overlay_tables (p, subdir->encoding_types,
parent_dir->encoding_types);

return new;
}
```

As a note -- if there is no per-directory merge function present, the server will just use the subdirectory's configuration info, and ignore the parent's. For some modules, that works just fine (*e.g.*, for the includes module, whose per-directory configuration information consists solely of the state of the XBITHACK), and for those modules, you can just not declare one, and leave the corresponding structure slot in the module itself NULL.

Command handling

Now that we have these structures, we need to be able to figure out how to fill them. That involves processing the actual AddType and AddEncoding commands. To find commands, the server looks in the module's command table. That table contains information on how many arguments the commands take, and in what formats, where it is permitted, and so forth. That information is sufficient to allow the server to invoke most command-handling functions with pre-parsed arguments. Without further ado, let's look at the AddType command handler, which looks like this (the AddEncoding command looks basically the same, and won't be shown here):

```
char *add_type(cmd_parms *cmd, mime_dir_config *m, char *ct, char *ext)
{
if (*ext == '.') ++ext;
ap_table_set (m->forced_types, ext, ct);
return NULL;
}
```

This command handler is unusually simple. As you can see, it takes four arguments, two of which are pre-parsed arguments, the third being the per-directory configuration structure for the module in question, and the fourth being a pointer to a cmd_parms structure. That structure contains a bunch of arguments which are frequently of use to some, but not all, commands, including a resource pool (from which memory can be allocated, and to which cleanups should be tied), and the (virtual) server being configured, from which the module's per-server configuration data can be obtained if required.

Another way in which this particular command handler is unusually simple is that there are no error conditions which it can encounter. If there were, it could return an error message instead of NULL; this causes an error to be printed out on the server's stderr, followed by a quick exit, if it is in the main config files; for a .htaccess file, the syntax error is logged in the server error log (along with an indication of where it came from), and the request is bounced with a server error response (HTTP error status, code 500).

The MIME module's command table has entries for these commands, which look like this:

```
command_rec mime_cmds[] = {
{ "AddType", add_type, NULL, OR_FILEINFO, TAKE2,
"a mime type followed by a file extension" },
{ "AddEncoding", add_encoding, NULL, OR_FILEINFO, TAKE2,
"an encoding (e.g., gzip), followed by a file extension" },
{ NULL }
};
```

The entries in these tables are:

- The name of the command
- The function which handles it
- a (void *) pointer, which is passed in the cmd_parms structure to the command handler --- this is useful in case many similar commands are handled by the same function.
- A bit mask indicating where the command may appear. There are mask bits corresponding to each AllowOverride option, and an additional mask bit, RSRC_CONF, indicating that the command may appear in the server's own config files, but *not* in any .htaccess file.
- A flag indicating how many arguments the command handler wants pre-parsed, and how they should be passed in. TAKE2 indicates two pre-parsed arguments. Other options are TAKE1, which indicates one pre-parsed argument, FLAG, which indicates that the argument should be On or Off, and is passed in as a boolean flag, RAW_ARGS, which causes the server to give the command the raw, unparsed arguments (everything but the command name itself). There is also ITERATE, which means that the handler looks the same as TAKE1, but that if multiple arguments are present, it should be called multiple times, and finally ITERATE2, which indicates that the command handler looks like a TAKE2, but if more arguments are present, then it should be called multiple times, holding the first argument constant.
- Finally, we have a string which describes the arguments that should be present. If the arguments in the actual config file are not as required, this string will be used to help give a more specific error message. (You can safely leave this NULL).

Finally, having set this all up, we have to use it. This is ultimately done in the module's handlers, specifically for its file-typing handler, which looks more or less like this; note that the per-directory configuration structure is extracted from the `request_rec`'s per-directory configuration vector by using the `ap_get_module_config` function.

```
int find_ct(request_rec *r)
{
int i;
char *fn = ap_pstrdup (r->pool, r->filename);
mime_dir_config *conf = (mime_dir_config *)
ap_get_module_config(r->per_dir_config, &mime_module);
char *type;

if (S_ISDIR(r->finfo.st_mode)) {
r->content_type = DIR_MAGIC_TYPE;
return OK;
}

if((i=ap_rind(fn,'.')) < 0) return DECLINED;
++i;

if ((type = ap_table_get (conf->encoding_types, &fn[i])))
{
r->content_encoding = type;

/* go back to previous extension to try to use it as a type */
fn[i-1] = '\0';
if((i=ap_rind(fn,'.')) < 0) return OK;
++i;
}

if ((type = ap_table_get (conf->forced_types, &fn[i])))
{
r->content_type = type;
}

return OK; }
```

Side notes -- per-server configuration, virtual servers, *etc.*

The basic ideas behind per-server module configuration are basically the same as those for per-directory configuration; there is a creation function and a merge function, the latter being invoked where a virtual server has partially overridden the base server configuration, and a combined structure must be computed. (As with per-directory configuration, the default if no merge function is specified, and a module is configured in some virtual server, is that the base configuration is simply ignored).

The only substantial difference is that when a command needs to configure the per-server private module data, it needs to go to the `cmd_parms` data to get at it. Here's an example, from the alias module, which also indicates how a syntax error can be returned (note that the per-directory configuration argument to the command handler is declared as a dummy, since the module doesn't actually have per-directory config data):

```
char *add_redirect(cmd_parms *cmd, void *dummy, char *f, char *url)
{
server_rec *s = cmd->server;
alias_server_conf *conf = (alias_server_conf *)
ap_get_module_config(s->module_config,&alias_module);
alias_entry *new = ap_push_array (conf->redirects);

if (!ap_is_url (url)) return "Redirect to non-URL";

new->fake = f; new->real = url;
return NULL;
}
```

Chapter 72.
Debugging Memory Allocation in APR

The allocation mechanisms within APR have a number of debugging modes that can be used to assist in finding memory problems. This document describes the modes available and gives instructions on activating them.

72.1. Available debugging options

Allocation Debugging - ALLOC_DEBUG

Debugging support: Define this to enable code which helps detect re-use of `free()`d memory and other such nonsense.

The theory is simple. The `FILL_BYTE` (0xa5) is written over all `malloc`'d memory as we receive it, and is written over everything that we free up during a `clear_pool`. We check that blocks on the free list always have the `FILL_BYTE` in them, and we check during `palloc()` that the bytes still have `FILL_BYTE` in them. If you ever see garbage URLs or whatnot containing lots of `0xa5`s then you know something used data that's been freed or uninitialized.

Malloc Support - ALLOC_USE_MALLOC

If defined all allocations will be done with `malloc()` and `free()`d appropriately at the end.

This is intended to be used with something like Electric Fence or Purify to help detect memory problems. Note that if you're using efence then you should also add in `ALLOC_DEBUG`. But don't add in `ALLOC_DEBUG` if you're using Purify because `ALLOC_DEBUG` would hide all the uninitialized read errors that Purify can diagnose.

Pool Debugging - POOL_DEBUG

This is intended to detect cases where the wrong pool is used when assigning data to an object in another pool.

In particular, it causes the `table_{set,add,merge}n` routines to check that their arguments are safe for the `apr_table_t` they're being placed in. It currently only works with the unix multiprocess model, but could be extended to others.

Table Debugging - MAKE_TABLE_PROFILE

Provide diagnostic information about make_table() calls which are possibly too small.

This requires a recent gcc which supports `__builtin_return_address()`. The error_log output will be a message such as:

```
table_push: apr_table_t created by 0x804d874 hit limit of 10
```

Use `l *0x804d874` to find the source that corresponds to. It indicates that a `apr_table_t` allocated by a call at that address has possibly too small an initial `apr_table_t` size guess.

Allocation Statistics - ALLOC_STATS

Provide some statistics on the cost of allocations.

This requires a bit of an understanding of how `alloc.c` works.

72.2. Allowable Combinations

Not all the options outlined above can be activated at the same time. the following table gives more information.

	ALLOC DEBUG	ALLOC USE MALLOC	POOL DEBUG	MAKE TABLE PROFILE	ALLOC STATS
ALLOC DEBUG	-	No	Yes	Yes	Yes
ALLOC USE MALLOC	No	-	No	No	No
POOL DEBUG	Yes	No	-	Yes	Yes
MAKE TABLE PROFILE	Yes	No	Yes	-	Yes
ALLOC STATS	Yes	No	Yes	Yes	-

Additionally the debugging options are not suitable for multi-threaded versions of the server. When trying to debug with these options the server should be started in single process mode.

72.3. Activating Debugging Options

The various options for debugging memory are now enabled in the `apr_general.h` header file in APR. The various options are enabled by uncommenting the define for the option you wish to use. The section of the code currently looks like this (*contained in srclib/apr/include/apr_pools.h*)

```
/*
#define ALLOC_DEBUG
#define POOL_DEBUG
#define ALLOC_USE_MALLOC
#define MAKE_TABLE_PROFILE
#define ALLOC_STATS
*/

typedef struct ap_pool_t {
union block_hdr *first;
union block_hdr *last;
struct cleanup *cleanups;
struct process_chain *subprocesses;
struct ap_pool_t *sub_pools;
struct ap_pool_t *sub_next;
struct ap_pool_t *sub_prev;
struct ap_pool_t *parent;
char *free_first_avail;
#ifdef ALLOC_USE_MALLOC
void *allocation_list;
#endif
#ifdef POOL_DEBUG
struct ap_pool_t *joined;
#endif
int (*apr_abort)(int retcode);
struct datastruct *prog_data;
} ap_pool_t;
```

To enable allocation debugging simply move the #define ALLOC_DEBUG above the start of the comments block and rebuild the server.

 Note

In order to use the various options the server **must** be rebuilt after editing the header file.

Chapter 73.
Documenting Apache 2.0

Apache 2.0 uses *Doxygen*[1] to document the APIs and global variables in the code. This will explain the basics of how to document using Doxygen.

73.1. Brief Description

To start a documentation block, use /**
To end a documentation block, use */

In the middle of the block, there are multiple tags we can use:

```
Description of this functions purpose
@param parameter_name description
@return description
@deffunc signature of the function
```

The deffunc is not always necessary. DoxyGen does not have a full parser in it, so any prototype that use a macro in the return type declaration is too complex for scandoc. Those functions require a deffunc. An example (using > rather than >):

```
/**
 * return the final element of the pathname
 * @param pathname The path to get the final element of
 * @return the final element of the path
 * @tip Examples:
 * <pre>
 * "/foo/bar/gum" -&gt; "gum"
 * "/foo/bar/gum/" -&gt; ""
 * "gum" -&gt; "gum"
 * "wi\\n32\\stuff" -&gt; "stuff"
 * </pre>
 * @deffunc const char * ap_filename_of_pathname(const char *pathname)
 */
```

At the top of the header file, always include:

---

[1] *http://www.doxygen.org/*

```
/**
 * @package Name of library header
 */
```

Doxygen uses a new HTML file for each package. The HTML files are named
{Name_of_library_header}.html, so try to be concise with your names.

For a further discussion of the possibilities please refer to *the Doxygen site*[2].

---

[2] *http://www.doxygen.org/*

Chapter 74.
Apache 2.0 Hook Functions

 Warning

This document is still in development and may be partially out of date.

In general, a hook function is one that Apache will call at some point during the processing of a request. Modules can provide functions that are called, and specify when they get called in comparison to other modules.

74.1. Creating a hook function

In order to create a new hook, four things need to be done:

Declare the hook function

Use the `AP_DECLARE_HOOK` macro, which needs to be given the return type of the hook function, the name of the hook, and the arguments. For example, if the hook returns an `int` and takes a `request_rec *` and an `int` and is called `do_something`, then declare it like this:

```
AP_DECLARE_HOOK(int, do_something, (request_rec *r, int n))
```

This should go in a header which modules will include if they want to use the hook.

Create the hook structure

Each source file that exports a hook has a private structure which is used to record the module functions that use the hook. This is declared as follows:

```
APR_HOOK_STRUCT(
APR_HOOK_LINK(do_something)
...
)
```

Implement the hook caller

The source file that exports the hook has to implement a function that will call the hook. There are currently three possible ways to do this. In all cases, the calling function is called `ap_run_hookname()`.

Void hooks

If the return value of a hook is `void`, then all the hooks are called, and the caller is implemented like this:

```
AP_IMPLEMENT_HOOK_VOID(do_something, (request_rec *r, int n), (r, n))
```

The second and third arguments are the dummy argument declaration and the dummy arguments as they will be used when calling the hook. In other words, this macro expands to something like this:

```
void ap_run_do_something(request_rec *r, int n)
{
...
do_something(r, n);
}
```

Hooks that return a value

If the hook returns a value, then it can either be run until the first hook that does something interesting, like so:

```
AP_IMPLEMENT_HOOK_RUN_FIRST(int, do_something, (request_rec *r, int n), (r, n),
DECLINED)
```

The first hook that does *not* return `DECLINED` stops the loop and its return value is returned from the hook caller. Note that `DECLINED` is the tradition Apache hook return meaning "I didn't do anything", but it can be whatever suits you.

Alternatively, all hooks can be run until an error occurs. This boils down to permitting *two* return values, one of which means "I did something, and it was OK" and the other meaning "I did nothing". The first function that returns a value other than one of those two stops the loop, and its return is the return value. Declare these like so:

```
AP_IMPLEMENT_HOOK_RUN_ALL(int, do_something, (request_rec *r, int n), (r, n), OK,
DECLINED)
```

Again, `OK` and `DECLINED` are the traditional values. You can use what you want.

Call the hook callers

At appropriate moments in the code, call the hook caller, like so:

```
int n, ret;
request_rec *r;

ret=ap_run_do_something(r, n);
```

74.2. Hooking the hook

A module that wants a hook to be called needs to do two things.

Implement the hook function

Include the appropriate header, and define a static function of the correct type:

```
static int my_something_doer(request_rec *r, int n)
{
...
return OK;
}
```

Add a hook registering function

During initialisation, Apache will call each modules hook registering function, which is included in the module structure:

```
static void my_register_hooks()
{
ap_hook_do_something(my_something_doer, NULL, NULL, APR_HOOK_MIDDLE);
}

mode MODULE_VAR_EXPORT my_module =
{
...
my_register_hooks /* register hooks */
};
```

Controlling hook calling order

In the example above, we didn't use the three arguments in the hook registration function that control calling order. There are two mechanisms for doing this. The first, rather crude, method, allows us to specify roughly where the hook is run relative to other modules. The final argument control this. There are three possible values: APR_HOOK_FIRST, APR_HOOK_MIDDLE and APR_HOOK_LAST.

All modules using any particular value may be run in any order relative to each other, but, of course, all modules using APR_HOOK_FIRST will be run before APR_HOOK_MIDDLE which are before APR_HOOK_LAST. Modules that don't care when they are run should use APR_HOOK_MIDDLE. (I spaced these out so people could do stuff like APR_HOOK_FIRST-2 to get in slightly earlier, but is this wise? - Ben)

Note that there are two more values, `APR_HOOK_REALLY_FIRST` and `APR_HOOK_REALLY_LAST`. These should only be used by the hook exporter.

The other method allows finer control. When a module knows that it must be run before (or after) some other modules, it can specify them by name. The second (third) argument is a NULL-terminated array of strings consisting of the names of modules that must be run before (after) the current module. For example, suppose we want "mod_xyz.c" and "mod_abc.c" to run before we do, then we'd hook as follows:

```
static void register_hooks()
{
static const char * const aszPre[] = { "mod_xyz.c", "mod_abc.c", NULL };

ap_hook_do_something(my_something_doer, aszPre, NULL, APR_HOOK_MIDDLE);
}
```

Note that the sort used to achieve this is stable, so ordering set by `APR_HOOK_ORDER` is preserved, as far as is possible.

Ben Laurie, 15th August 1999

Chapter 75.

Converting Modules from Apache 1.3 to Apache 2.0

This is a first attempt at writing the lessons I learned when trying to convert the `mod_mmap_static` module to Apache 2.0. It's by no means definitive and probably won't even be correct in some ways, but it's a start.

75.1. The easier changes ...

Cleanup Routines

These now need to be of type `apr_status_t` and return a value of that type. Normally the return value will be `APR_SUCCESS` unless there is some need to signal an error in the cleanup. Be aware that even though you signal an error not all code yet checks and acts upon the error.

Initialisation Routines

These should now be renamed to better signify where they sit in the overall process. So the name gets a small change from `mmap_init` to `mmap_post_config`. The arguments passed have undergone a radical change and now look like

- `apr_pool_t *p`
- `apr_pool_t *plog`
- `apr_pool_t *ptemp`
- `server_rec *s`

Data Types

A lot of the data types have been moved into the *APR*[1]. This means that some have had a name change, such as the one shown above. The following is a brief list of some of the changes that you are likely to have to make.

---

[1] *http://apr.apache.org/*

- `pool` becomes `apr_pool_t`
- `table` becomes `apr_table_t`

75.2. The messier changes...

Register Hooks

The new architecture uses a series of hooks to provide for calling your functions. These you'll need to add to your module by way of a new function, `static void register_hooks(void)`. The function is really reasonably straightforward once you understand what needs to be done. Each function that needs calling at some stage in the processing of a request needs to be registered, handlers do not. There are a number of phases where functions can be added, and for each you can specify with a high degree of control the relative order that the function will be called in.

This is the code that was added to `mod_mmap_static`:

```
static void register_hooks(void)
{
    static const char * const aszPre[]={ "http_core.c",NULL };
    ap_hook_post_config(mmap_post_config,NULL,NULL,HOOK_MIDDLE);
    ap_hook_translate_name(mmap_static_xlat,aszPre,NULL,HOOK_LAST);
};
```

This registers 2 functions that need to be called, one in the `post_config` stage (virtually every module will need this one) and one for the `translate_name` phase. note that while there are different function names the format of each is identical. So what is the format?

```
ap_hook_phase_name(function_name, predecessors, successors, position);
```

There are 3 hook positions defined...

- `HOOK_FIRST`
- `HOOK_MIDDLE`
- `HOOK_LAST`

To define the position you use the position and then modify it with the predecessors and successors. Each of the modifiers can be a list of functions that should be called, either before the function is run (predecessors) or after the function has run (successors).

In the `mod_mmap_static` case I didn't care about the `post_config` stage, but the `mmap_static_xlat` **must** be called after the core module had done it's name translation, hence the use of the aszPre to define a modifier to the position `HOOK_LAST`.

Module Definition

There are now a lot fewer stages to worry about when creating your module definition. The old defintion looked like

```
module MODULE_VAR_EXPORT module_name_module =
{
    STANDARD_MODULE_STUFF,
    /* initializer */
    /* dir config creater */
    /* dir merger --- default is to override */
    /* server config */
    /* merge server config */
    /* command handlers */
    /* handlers */
    /* filename translation */
    /* check_user_id */
    /* check auth */
    /* check access */
    /* type_checker */
    /* fixups */
    /* logger */
    /* header parser */
    /* child_init */
    /* child_exit */
    /* post read-request */
};
```

The new structure is a great deal simpler...

```
module MODULE_VAR_EXPORT module_name_module =
{
    STANDARD20_MODULE_STUFF,
    /* create per-directory config structures */
    /* merge per-directory config structures  */
    /* create per-server config structures    */
    /* merge per-server config structures     */
    /* command handlers */
    /* handlers */
    /* register hooks */
};
```

Some of these read directly across, some don't. I'll try to summarise what should be done below.

The stages that read directly across :

```
/* dir config creater */
```
```
    /* create per-directory config structures */
```
```
/* server config */
```
```
    /* create per-server config structures */
```

```
/* dir merger */
```

    `/* merge per-directory config structures */`

```
/* merge server config */
```

    `/* merge per-server config structures */`

```
/* command table */
```

    `/* command apr_table_t */`

```
/* handlers */
```

    `/* handlers */`

The remainder of the old functions should be registered as hooks. There are the following hook stages defined so far...

`ap_hook_post_config`

    this is where the old _init routines get registered

`ap_hook_http_method`

    retrieve the http method from a request. (legacy)

`ap_hook_open_logs`

    open any specified logs

`ap_hook_auth_checker`

    check if the resource requires authorization

`ap_hook_access_checker`

    check for module-specific restrictions

`ap_hook_check_user_id`

    check the user-id and password

`ap_hook_default_port`

    retrieve the default port for the server

`ap_hook_pre_connection`

    do any setup required just before processing, but after accepting

`ap_hook_process_connection`

    run the correct protocol

`ap_hook_child_init`

    call as soon as the child is started

`ap_hook_create_request`

   ??

`ap_hook_fixups`

   last chance to modify things before generating content

`ap_hook_handler`

   generate the content

`ap_hook_header_parser`

   lets modules look at the headers, not used by most modules, because they use
   `post_read_request` for this

`ap_hook_insert_filter`

   to insert filters into the filter chain

`ap_hook_log_transaction`

   log information about the request

`ap_hook_optional_fn_retrieve`

   retrieve any functions registered as optional

`ap_hook_post_read_request`

   called after reading the request, before any other phase

`ap_hook_quick_handler`

   called before any request processing, used by cache modules.

`ap_hook_translate_name`

   translate the URI into a filename

`ap_hook_type_checker`

   determine and/or set the doc type

Chapter 76.

Request Processing in Apache 2.0

 Warning

Warning - this is a first (fast) draft that needs further revision!

Several changes in Apache 2.0 affect the internal request processing mechanics. Module authors need to be aware of these changes so they may take advantage of the optimizations and security enhancements.

The first major change is to the subrequest and redirect mechanisms. There were a number of different code paths in Apache 1.3 to attempt to optimize subrequest or redirect behavior. As patches were introduced to 2.0, these optimizations (and the server behavior) were quickly broken due to this duplication of code. All duplicate code has been folded back into `ap_process_request_internal()` to prevent the code from falling out of sync again.

This means that much of the existing code was 'unoptimized'. It is the Apache HTTP Project's first goal to create a robust and correct implementation of the HTTP server RFC. Additional goals include security, scalability and optimization. New methods were sought to optimize the server (beyond the performance of Apache 1.3) without introducing fragile or insecure code.

76.1. The Request Processing Cycle

All requests pass through `ap_process_request_internal()` in `request.c`, including subrequests and redirects. If a module doesn't pass generated requests through this code, the author is cautioned that the module may be broken by future changes to request processing.

To streamline requests, the module author can take advantage of the hooks offered to drop out of the request cycle early, or to bypass core Apache hooks which are irrelevant (and costly in terms of CPU.)

76.2. The Request Parsing Phase

Unescapes the URL

The request's `parsed_uri` path is unescaped, once and only once, at the beginning of internal request processing.

This step is bypassed if the proxyreq flag is set, or the `parsed_uri.path` element is unset. The module has no further control of this one-time unescape operation, either failing to unescape or multiply unescaping the URL leads to security reprecussions.

Strips Parent and This Elements from the URI

All `/../` and `/./` elements are removed by `ap_getparents()`. This helps to ensure the path is (nearly) absolute before the request processing continues.

This step cannot be bypassed.

Initial URI Location Walk

Every request is subject to an `ap_location_walk()` call. This ensures that `<Location>` sections are consistently enforced for all requests. If the request is an internal redirect or a sub-request, it may borrow some or all of the processing from the previous or parent request's ap_location_walk, so this step is generally very efficient after processing the main request.

translate_name

Modules can determine the file name, or alter the given URI in this step. For example, `mod_vhost_alias` will translate the URI's path into the configured virtual host, `mod_alias` will translate the path to an alias path, and if the request falls back on the core, the `DocumentRoot` is prepended to the request resource.

If all modules DECLINE this phase, an error 500 is returned to the browser, and a "couldn't translate name" error is logged automatically.

Hook: map_to_storage

After the file or correct URI was determined, the appropriate per-dir configurations are merged together. For example, `mod_proxy` compares and merges the appropriate `<Proxy>` sections. If the URI is nothing more than a local (non-proxy) TRACE request, the core handles the request and returns DONE. If no module answers this hook with OK or DONE, the core will run the request filename against the `<Directory>` and `<Files>` sections. If the request 'filename' isn't an absolute, legal filename, a note is set for later termination.

URI Location Walk

Every request is hardened by a second `ap_location_walk()` call. This reassures that a translated request is still subjected to the configured `<Location>` sections. The request again borrows some or all of the processing from its previous `location_walk` above, so this step is almost always very efficient unless the translated URI mapped to a substantially different path or Virtual Host.

Hook: header_parser

The main request then parses the client's headers. This prepares the remaining request processing steps to better serve the client's request.

76.3. The Security Phase

Needs Documentation. Code is:

```
switch (ap_satisfies(r)) {
case SATISFY_ALL:
case SATISFY_NOSPEC:
    if ((access_status = ap_run_access_checker(r)) != 0) {
        return decl_die(access_status, "check access", r);
    }

    if (ap_some_auth_required(r)) {
        if (((access_status = ap_run_check_user_id(r)) != 0)
            || !ap_auth_type(r)) {
            return decl_die(access_status, ap_auth_type(r)
                            ? "check user.  No user file?"
                            : "perform authentication. AuthType not set!",
                            r);
        }

        if (((access_status = ap_run_auth_checker(r)) != 0)
            || !ap_auth_type(r)) {
            return decl_die(access_status, ap_auth_type(r)
                            ? "check access.  No groups file?"
                            : "perform authentication. AuthType not set!",
                            r);
        }
    }
    break;

case SATISFY_ANY:
    if (((access_status = ap_run_access_checker(r)) != 0)) {
        if (!ap_some_auth_required(r)) {
            return decl_die(access_status, "check access", r);
        }

        if (((access_status = ap_run_check_user_id(r)) != 0)
```

```
            || !ap_auth_type(r)) {
            return decl_die(access_status, ap_auth_type(r)
                        ? "check user.  No user file?"
                        : "perform authentication. AuthType not set!",
                        r);
        }

        if (((access_status = ap_run_auth_checker(r)) != 0)
            || !ap_auth_type(r)) {
            return decl_die(access_status, ap_auth_type(r)
                        ? "check access.  No groups file?"
                        : "perform authentication. AuthType not set!",
                        r);
        }
    }
    break;
}
```

76.4. The Preparation Phase

Hook: type_checker

The modules have an opportunity to test the URI or filename against the target resource, and set mime information for the request. Both <u>mod mime</u> and <u>mod mime magic</u> use this phase to compare the file name or contents against the administrator's configuration and set the content type, language, character set and request handler. Some modules may set up their filters or other request handling parameters at this time.

If all modules DECLINE this phase, an error 500 is returned to the browser, and a "couldn't find types" error is logged automatically.

Hook: fixups

Many modules are 'trounced' by some phase above. The fixups phase is used by modules to 'reassert' their ownership or force the request's fields to their appropriate values. It isn't always the cleanest mechanism, but occasionally it's the only option.

76.5. The Handler Phase

This phase is **not** part of the processing in ap_process_request_internal(). Many modules prepare one or more subrequests prior to creating any content at all. After the core, or a module calls ap_process_request_internal() it then calls ap_invoke_handler() to generate the request.

Hook: insert_filter

Modules that transform the content in some way can insert their values and override existing filters, such that if the user configured a more advanced filter out-of-order, then the module can move its order as need be. There is no result code, so actions in this hook better be trusted to always succeed.

Hook: handler

The module finally has a chance to serve the request in its handler hook. Note that not every prepared request is sent to the handler hook. Many modules, such as mod_autoindex, will create subrequests for a given URI, and then never serve the subrequest, but simply lists it for the user. Remember not to put required teardown from the hooks above into this module, but register pool cleanups against the request pool to free resources as required.

Chapter 77.

How filters work in Apache 2.0

 Warning

This is a cut 'n paste job from an email (<022501c1c529$f63a9550$7f00000a@KOJ>) and only reformatted for better readability. It's not up to date but may be a good start for further research.

77.1. Filter Types

There are three basic filter types (each of these is actually broken down into two categories, but that comes later).

CONNECTION

Filters of this type are valid for the lifetime of this connection. (`AP_FTYPE_CONNECTION`, `AP_FTYPE_NETWORK`)

PROTOCOL

Filters of this type are valid for the lifetime of this request from the point of view of the client, this means that the request is valid from the time that the request is sent until the time that the response is received. (`AP_FTYPE_PROTOCOL`, `AP_FTYPE_TRANSCODE`)

RESOURCE

Filters of this type are valid for the time that this content is used to satisfy a request. For simple requests, this is identical to `PROTOCOL`, but internal redirects and sub-requests can change the content without ending the request. (`AP_FTYPE_RESOURCE`, `AP_FTYPE_CONTENT_SET`)

It is important to make the distinction between a protocol and a resource filter. A resource filter is tied to a specific resource, it may also be tied to header information, but the main binding is to a resource. If you are writing a filter and you want to know if it is resource or protocol, the correct question to ask is: "Can this filter be removed if the request is redirected to a different resource?" If the answer is yes, then it is a resource filter. If it is no, then it is most likely a protocol or connection filter. I won't go into connection filters, because they seem to be well understood. With this definition, a few examples might help:

Byterange

We have coded it to be inserted for all requests, and it is removed if not used. Because this filter is active at the beginning of all requests, it can not be removed if it is redirected, so this is a protocol filter.

http_header

This filter actually writes the headers to the network. This is obviously a required filter (except in the asis case which is special and will be dealt with below) and so it is a protocol filter.

Deflate

The administrator configures this filter based on which file has been requested. If we do an internal redirect from an autoindex page to an index.html page, the deflate filter may be added or removed based on config, so this is a resource filter.

The further breakdown of each category into two more filter types is strictly for ordering. We could remove it, and only allow for one filter type, but the order would tend to be wrong, and we would need to hack things to make it work. Currently, the RESOURCE filters only have one filter type, but that should change.

77.2. How are filters inserted?

This is actually rather simple in theory, but the code is complex. First of all, it is important that everybody realize that there are three filter lists for each request, but they are all concatenated together. So, the first list is r->output_filters, then r->proto_output_filters, and finally r->connection->output_filters. These correspond to the RESOURCE, PROTOCOL, and CONNECTION filters respectively. The problem previously, was that we used a singly linked list to create the filter stack, and we started from the "correct" location. This means that if I had a RESOURCE filter on the stack, and I added a CONNECTION filter, the CONNECTION filter would be ignored. This should make sense, because we would insert the connection filter at the top of the c->output_filters list, but the end of r->output_filters pointed to the filter that used to be at the front of c->output_filters. This is obviously wrong. The new insertion code uses a doubly linked list. This has the advantage that we never lose a filter that has been inserted. Unfortunately, it comes with a separate set of headaches.

The problem is that we have two different cases were we use subrequests. The first is to insert more data into a response. The second is to replace the existing response with an internal redirect. These are two different cases and need to be treated as such.

In the first case, we are creating the subrequest from within a handler or filter. This means that the next filter should be passed to make_sub_request function, and the last resource filter in the sub-request will point to the next filter in the main request. This makes sense, because the sub-request's data needs to flow through the same set of filters as the main request. A graphical representation might help:

```
Default_handler --> includes_filter --> byterange --> ...
```

If the includes filter creates a sub request, then we don't want the data from that sub-request to go through the includes filter, because it might not be SSI data. So, the subrequest adds the following:

```
Default_handler --> includes_filter -/-> byterange --> ...
                                    /
Default_handler --> sub_request_core
```

What happens if the subrequest is SSI data? Well, that's easy, the includes_filter is a resource filter, so it will be added to the sub request in between the Default_handler and the sub_request_core filter.

The second case for sub-requests is when one sub-request is going to become the real request. This happens whenever a sub-request is created outside of a handler or filter, and NULL is passed as the next filter to the make_sub_request function.

In this case, the resource filters no longer make sense for the new request, because the resource has changed. So, instead of starting from scratch, we simply point the front of the resource filters for the sub-request to the front of the protocol filters for the old request. This means that we won't lose any of the protocol filters, neither will we try to send this data through a filter that shouldn't see it.

The problem is that we are using a doubly-linked list for our filter stacks now. But, you should notice that it is possible for two lists to intersect in this model. So, you do you handle the previous pointer? This is a very difficult question to answer, because there is no "right" answer, either method is equally valid. I looked at why we use the previous pointer. The only reason for it is to allow for easier addition of new servers. With that being said, the solution I chose was to make the previous pointer always stay on the original request.

This causes some more complex logic, but it works for all cases. My concern in having it move to the sub-request, is that for the more common case (where a sub-request is used to add data to a response), the main filter chain would be wrong. That didn't seem like a good idea to me.

77.3. Asis

The final topic. :-) Mod_Asis is a bit of a hack, but the handler needs to remove all filters except for connection filters, and send the data. If you are using mod_asis, all other bets are off.

77.4. Explanations

The absolutely last point is that the reason this code was so hard to get right, was because we had hacked so much to force it to work. I wrote most of the hacks originally, so I am very much to blame. However, now that the code is right, I have started to remove some hacks. Most people should have seen that the `reset_filters` and `add_required_filters` functions are gone. Those inserted protocol level filters for error conditions, in fact, both functions did the same thing, one after the other, it was really strange. Because we don't lose protocol filters for error cases any more, those hacks went away. The `HTTP_HEADER`, `Content-length`, and `Byterange` filters are all added in the `insert_filters` phase, because if they were added earlier, we had some interesting interactions. Now, those could all be moved to be inserted with the `HTTP_IN`, `CORE`, and `CORE_IN` filters. That would make the code easier to follow.

Chapter 78.
Apache 2.0 Thread Safety Issues

When using any of the threaded mpms in Apache 2.0 it is important that every function called from Apache be thread safe. When linking in 3rd party extensions it can be difficult to determine whether the resulting server will be thread safe. Casual testing generally won't tell you this either as thread safety problems can lead to subtle race conditons that may only show up in certain conditions under heavy load.

78.1. Global and static variables

When writing your module or when trying to determine if a module or 3rd party library is thread safe there are some common things to keep in mind.

First, you need to recognize that in a threaded model each individual thread has its own program counter, stack and registers. Local variables live on the stack, so those are fine. You need to watch out for any static or global variables. This doesn't mean that you are absolutely not allowed to use static or global variables. There are times when you actually want something to affect all threads, but generally you need to avoid using them if you want your code to be thread safe.

In the case where you have a global variable that needs to be global and accessed by all threads, be very careful when you update it. If, for example, it is an incrementing counter, you need to atomically increment it to avoid race conditions with other threads. You do this using a mutex (mutual exclusion). Lock the mutex, read the current value, increment it and write it back and then unlock the mutex. Any other thread that wants to modify the value has to first check the mutex and block until it is cleared.

If you are using *APR*[1], have a look at the `apr_atomic_*` functions and the `apr_thread_mutex_*` functions.

78.2. errno

This is a common global variable that holds the error number of the last error that occurred. If one thread calls a low-level function that sets errno and then another thread checks it, we

---

[1] *http://apr.apache.org/*

are bleeding error numbers from one thread into another. To solve this, make sure your module or library defines _REENTRANT or is compiled with -D_REENTRANT. This will make errno a per-thread variable and should hopefully be transparent to the code. It does this by doing something like this:

```
#define errno (*(__errno_location()))
```

which means that accessing errno will call __errno_location() which is provided by the libc. Setting _REENTRANT also forces redefinition of some other functions to their *_r equivalents and sometimes changes the common getc/putc macros into safer function calls. Check your libc documentation for specifics. Instead of, or in addition to _REENTRANT the symbols that may affect this are _POSIX_C_SOURCE, _THREAD_SAFE, _SVID_SOURCE, and _BSD_SOURCE.

78.3. Common standard troublesome functions

Not only do things have to be thread safe, but they also have to be reentrant. strtok() is an obvious one. You call it the first time with your delimiter which it then remembers and on each subsequent call it returns the next token. Obviously if multiple threads are calling it you will have a problem. Most systems have a reentrant version of of the function called strtok_r() where you pass in an extra argument which contains an allocated char * which the function will use instead of its own static storage for maintaining the tokenizing state. If you are using *APR*[2] you can use apr_strtok().

crypt() is another function that tends to not be reentrant, so if you run across calls to that function in a library, watch out. On some systems it is reentrant though, so it is not always a problem. If your system has crypt_r() chances are you should be using that, or if possible simply avoid the whole mess by using md5 instead.

78.4. Common 3rd Party Libraries

The following is a list of common libraries that are used by 3rd party Apache modules. You can check to see if your module is using a potentially unsafe library by using tools such as ldd(1) and nm(1). For *PHP*[3], for example, try this:

```
% ldd libphp4.so
libsablot.so.0 => /usr/local/lib/libsablot.so.0 (0x401f6000)
libexpat.so.0 => /usr/lib/libexpat.so.0 (0x402da000)
libsnmp.so.0 => /usr/lib/libsnmp.so.0 (0x402f9000)
libpdf.so.1 => /usr/local/lib/libpdf.so.1 (0x40353000)
libz.so.1 => /usr/lib/libz.so.1 (0x403e2000)
```

---

[2] *http://apr.apache.org/*
[3] *http://www.php.net/*

```
libpng.so.2 => /usr/lib/libpng.so.2 (0x403f0000)
libmysqlclient.so.11 => /usr/lib/libmysqlclient.so.11 (0x40411000)
libming.so => /usr/lib/libming.so (0x40449000)
libm.so.6 => /lib/libm.so.6 (0x40487000)
libfreetype.so.6 => /usr/lib/libfreetype.so.6 (0x404a8000)
libjpeg.so.62 => /usr/lib/libjpeg.so.62 (0x404e7000)
libcrypt.so.1 => /lib/libcrypt.so.1 (0x40505000)
libssl.so.2 => /lib/libssl.so.2 (0x40532000)
libcrypto.so.2 => /lib/libcrypto.so.2 (0x40560000)
libresolv.so.2 => /lib/libresolv.so.2 (0x40624000)
libdl.so.2 => /lib/libdl.so.2 (0x40634000)
libnsl.so.1 => /lib/libnsl.so.1 (0x40637000)
libc.so.6 => /lib/libc.so.6 (0x4064b000)
/lib/ld-linux.so.2 => /lib/ld-linux.so.2 (0x80000000)
```

In addition to these libraries you will need to have a look at any libraries linked statically into the module. You can use nm(1) to look for individual symbols in the module.

78.5. Library List

Please drop a note to *dev@httpd.apache.org* if you have additions or corrections to this list.

Library	Version	Thread Safe?	Notes
ASpell/PSpell[4]		?	
Berkeley DB[5]	3.x, 4.x	Yes	Be careful about sharing a connection across threads.
bzip2[6]		Yes	Both low-level and high-level APIs are thread-safe. However, high-level API requires thread-safe access to errno.
cdb[7]		?	
C-Client[8]		Perhaps	c-client uses strtok() and gethostbyname() which are not thread-safe on most C library implementations. c-client's static data is meant to be shared across threads. If strtok() and gethostbyname() are thread-safe on your OS, c-client *may* be thread-safe.
libcrypt[9]		?	
Expat[10]		Yes	Need a separate parser instance per thread

[4] *http://aspell.sourceforge.net/*

[5] *http://www.sleepycat.com/*

[6] *http://sources.redhat.com/bzip2/index.html*

[7] *http://cr.yp.to/cdb.html*

[8] *http://www.washington.edu/imap/*

[9] *http://www.ijg.org/files/*

Library	Version	Thread Safe?	Notes
FreeTDS[11]		?	
FreeType[12]		?	
GD 1.8.x[13]		?	
GD 2.0.x[14]		?	
gdbm[15]		No	Errors returned via a static gdbm_error variable
ImageMagick[16]	5.2.2	Yes	ImageMagick docs claim it is thread safe since version 5.2.2 (see *Change log*[17]).
Imlib2[18]		?	
libjpeg[19]	v6b	?	
libmysqlclient[20]		Yes	Use mysqlclient_r library variant to ensure thread-safety. For more information, please read *http://dev.mysql.com/doc/mysql/en/Threaded_clients.html*.
Ming[21]	0.2a	?	
Net-SNMP[22]	5.0.x	?	
OpenLDAP[23]	2.1.x	Yes	Use ldap_r library variant to ensure thread-safety.
OpenSSL[24]	0.9.6g	Yes	Requires proper usage of CRYPTO_num_locks, CRYPTO_set_locking_callback, CRYPTO_set_id_callback
liboci8 (Oracle 8+)[25]	8.x,9.x	?	

[10] *http://expat.sourceforge.net/*

[11] *http://www.freetds.org/*

[12] *http://www.freetype.org/*

[13] *http://www.boutell.com/gd/*

[14] *http://www.boutell.com/gd/*

[15] *http://www.gnu.org/software/gdbm/gdbm.html*

[16] *http://www.imagemagick.org/*

[17] *http://www.imagemagick.com/www/changelog.html*

[18] *http://www.enlightenment.org/p.php?p=about/efl&l=en*

[19] *http://www.ijg.org/files/*

[20] *http://mysql.com/*

[21] *http://www.opaque.net/ming/*

[22] *http://net-snmp.sourceforge.net/*

[23] *http://www.openldap.org/*

[24] *http://www.openssl.org/*

[25] *http://www.oracle.com/*

Library	Version	Thread Safe?	Notes
pdflib[26]	5.0.x	Yes	PDFLib docs claim it is thread safe; changes.txt indicates it has been partially thread-safe since V1.91: *http://www.pdflib.com/products/pdflib-family/pdflib/.*
libpng[27]	1.0.x	?	
libpng[28]	1.2.x	?	
libpq (PostgreSQL)[29]	8.x	Yes	Don't share connections across threads and watch out for crypt() calls
Sablotron[30]	0.95	?	
zlib[31]	1.1.4	Yes	Relies upon thread-safe zalloc and zfree functions Default is to use libc's calloc/free which are thread-safe.

---

[26] *http://pdflib.com/*

[27] *http://www.libpng.org/pub/png/libpng.html*

[28] *http://www.libpng.org/pub/png/libpng.html*

[29] *http://www.postgresql.org/docs/8.4/static/libpq-threading.html*

[30] *http://www.gingerall.com/charlie/ga/xml/p_sab.xml*

[31] *http://www.gzip.org/zlib/*

Linbrary™ Advertising Club (LAC)

Linbrary™ Official Docs as a Real Books
http://www.linbrary.com   📚 Linux Library

Linbrary Advertising Club

CPSIA information can be obtained at www.ICGtesting.com
Printed in the USA
BVOW081503130112

280403BV00005B/11/P